CONTENTS

Title Page
Copyright
Introduction: How It All Started ... 1
Personal Story: Stumping Sav ... 10
Personal Story: A Special Radio Request ... 15
Album Spotlight: On Through The Night ... 18
Album Spotlight: High 'n' Dry ... 22
Album Spotlight: Pyromania ... 29
Album Spotlight: Hysteria ... 36
Steve Clark: A Tribute ... 49
Album Spotlight: Adrenalize ... 54
Album Spotlight: Retro Active ... 59
Peeks Inside Vault's Vault & More! ... 68
Album Spotlight: Slang ... 80
Album Spotlight: Euphoria ... 87
Album Spotlight: X ... 93
Album Spotlight: Songs From The Sparkle Lounge ... 103
Album Spotlight: Def Leppard ... 108
Personal Story: If It Pleases You, It Pleases...Them ... 118
Personal Story: An 'Ugly' Situation With A Concert On The Side ... 121

Personal Story: Definitely Not A Wardrobe Malfunction	126
Personal Story: Where Does Love Go When It Dies? Right Here!	131
Single Spotlight: "Women"	135
Single Spotlight: "Hysteria"	141
Single Spotlight: "Pour Some Sugar On Me"	146
Single Spotlight: "Love Bites"	152
Single Spotlight (And A Personal One At That!): "Rocket"	157
Single Spotlight: "Let's Get Rocked"	164
Single Spotlight: "Make Love Like A Man"	169
Single Spotlight: "Tonight"	175
Single Spotlight: "Promises"	179
Single Spotlight: "Long Long Way To Go"	184
Single Spotlight: "Nine Lives"	189
The Magical Mysteria Of "Mutt" Lange	194
Personal Story: Poor Sav...And Go, Joe!	225
Personal Story: And Now A Quick Break For The Scent Of Glitter	234
Personal Story: The Ballad Of Joe (Reflections & An Appreciation)	239
Personal Story: Meet. Greet. Repeat.	252
Ranking & Reviewing Def Leppard's Songs	261

I GOT SOMETHING TO SAY!

Collections, Recollections & Personal Reflections About Def Leppard

From The Creator Of The Def Leppard Fansite "The Lep Report" (DefLeppardReport.com)

Copyright © 2021 The Lep Report

All rights reserved

No part of this book may be reproduced, or stored in a retrieval system, or transmitted in any form or by any means, electronic, mechanical, photocopying, recording, or otherwise, without express written permission of the publisher.

Introduction: How It All Started

I said welcome to my...book!

I think it's safe to assume you're a Def Leppard fan. So am I -- big surprise, right? -- for as far back as I can remember.

If you're old enough, you likely recall when you first saw "Bringin' On The Heartbreak" on MTV or heard the one-of-a-kind "*Gunter, Gleiben, Glauten, Globen*" introduction to "Rock of Ages," or the stuttering yet catchy chorus of "Foolin'."

You probably also recall where you were and how you felt the first time you heard about Rick Allen's horrifying car crash, as well as the tragic death of Steve Clark, both of which occurred *way* before social media and widespread high-speed internet access so you'd be glued to MTV awaiting the latest news updates.

How about hearing *Pyromania* or *Hysteria* for the first time? Or "Pour Some Sugar On Me," which you quickly became accustomed to hearing all over radio stations in 1988, not to mention seeing its music video (the iconic U.S. concert version) reign supreme on MTV.

Or simply seeing the band live, be it your first or favorite Def Leppard concert.

These are all special moments that are not only memorable but meaningful for many, including me.

Def Leppard has a wonderful, enthusiastic fan base. Not just admirers, but deeply passionate fans who have an affinity for the group, with a personal interest in wanting the band to succeed.

Based on my own experiences and interactions with dedicated Def Leppard fans over the years (okay, decades), it's abundantly clear many have a great knowledge of the band, and are genuinely interested in topics that transcend simply having a favorite song or album.

I can relate and agree! There is absolutely a lot more beneath the surface to dissect and analyze when discussing Def Leppard's albums and songs. And that's exactly what I've set out to do with this book, with the hope that you'll find it entertaining and even enlightening.

Additionally, this book also includes some of my own favorite personal stories and behind-the-scenes interactions involving Def Leppard which I think you will enjoy, from the time I had the opportunity to work at the band's record label. I found the experience to be thrilling and filled with unforgettable memories -- especially as someone who grew up being such a big fan of the band (as I'm sure many of you are, too).

It may seem peculiar, but early on my interest in Def Leppard went beyond the final product, aka the music; it was about week-to-week radio airplay performance, sales chart performance, tour grosses and concert attendance by market (i.e., city), how the band's material, image, and overall brand was being marketed and promoted -- from the execution of a single or album's release strategy, to the creative direction of a song's music video, to how a tour was being positioned and advertised, and so on.

In general, all of these things *really* appealed to me, most especially about Def Leppard.

Of course, the music itself was most important, but these

other subjects had vital roles, like when a music video achieved heavy rotation during the "good ole days" of MTV.

Speaking of which, remember the show "Dial MTV," which would countdown the music videos that received the most votes from viewers (courtesy of an 800 number) each day? Yours truly had the opportunity to proudly introduce Def Leppard's "Armageddon It" video to MTV's audience (over the phone) back in 1989, an event I was fortunate to record on a VHS tape when it aired and still have in my collection.

I was a junior in high school around that time, and what was my favorite weekly routine? Going to record stores and magazine stands to read the latest issue of *Billboard* magazine and study the latest chart movements. Fun stuff, right? I ended up subscribing to that music industry publication, which cost a pretty penny! Surprisingly, I was never able to find other high school students who were fellow *Billboard* magazine subscribers. Shocking.

I would eagerly look forward to each issue, seeking where the latest debuts landed on the albums and singles charts, studying the current releases that were climbing and dropping, noting which ones possessed *Billboard*'s sought-after bullet symbol (an indication of not only maintaining but gaining chart momentum; that's also where the phrase "number one with a bullet" originates), etc.

Tedious information to many, no doubt, but something I found fascinating.

Tracking the *Hysteria* album's chart performance as it was actually happening in the late '80s, along with its numerous single releases and seemingly endless tour (seeing data that included concert grosses, venue capacity vs. actual attendance, etc.) was an intriguing exercise.

It was a thrill ride observing how *Hysteri*a would continually reside at the top of *Billboard*'s U.S. album chart, and reaching #1 on multiple occasions, even a year after its release!

My interest and dedication may have been a bit uncommon, but I embraced it, to the point I felt I could utilize that passion, in some shape or form, maybe incorporate it into my career or even, heck, somehow help Def Leppard -- no matter how minor the contribution -- along the way. Why not?! A high school kid can dream!

After high school, my focus in college ultimately centered around brand management and marketing, including music marketing, which involved learning the ins and outs of the music business. (Initially, I took a "music" class at a university in the early '90s which I thought included a curriculum that covered the "business side," but was sadly mistaken when on the first day a nun walked into the room and introduced herself as the instructor. She walked up to what looked like a century-old phonograph and placed the player's needle onto a vinyl record of old classical music. I dropped the class that day, and not long after, the university as well. I transferred to another college with classes that better synched up with my interests, so much so that I ended up writing an essay for one final exam that made the case for why Def Leppard should be inducted into the Rock & Roll Hall of Fame. A couple of decades premature, I guess.)

Adrenalize was released while I was in college, and I'm positive I wasn't the only one rooting for the band's triumphant return after Steve Clark's death. The album was a roaring success out of the box, debuting at #1 -- my issue of *Billboard* magazine confirmed it, too, which I still have today.

It was gratifying to see the band back in action and able to take that important, chart-topping victory lap. (In hindsight, *Adrenalize*'s sales momentum arguably could have lasted longer, something which will be discussed in the chapters spotlighting the album and its singles.)

As a fan simply observing things play out in 1992, I wished

I somehow could have been involved to help out, beyond just buying *Adrenalize* (as well as its cassingles, CD imports with bonus tracks, and so on).

I emphatically wondered what singles would be chosen for the album, and in what order; how their video counterparts would look and whether they would complement or detract from the song they represented; what their radio strategy was, and what station formats they would target; how the marketing and advertising campaigns would look, etc.

Sure, it was entertaining to witness from afar, but I didn't just want to be a bystander. The appeal of the music business made me want to become more involved, observe these things "from the inside" instead of only from the outside looking in.

So I did just that.

During my third year in college, I had the opportunity to work at the band's record distributor, and, as timing (and luck) would have it, the band's record label about halfway into the band's *Adrenalize* release and tour. My time there also included future Def Leppard releases *Vault*, *Retro Active*, and *Slang*.

I fondly recall the first time I walked through the record company's lobby doors, noticing a plaque on the wall featuring the bright, electric blue colors of the *Adrenalize* album cover, commemorating its multi-platinum certification. It felt comforting and surreal all at once, especially since my typical work routine was going to include not only Def Leppard-related projects but other acts as well, including Bon Jovi, Kiss, The Scorpions, Iron Maiden's Bruce Dickinson, just to name a few.

On a related note, goodbye *Billboard* subscription! Copies of the magazine were scattered throughout the office, in addition to several other industry publications that included a boatload of additional data to feast on, like *Radio & Records* ("R&R"), *The Album Network*, *Hits*, and so on. They all became part of my regular reading routine.

This was during a unique, transformative period for Def Leppard. The heyday of *Hysteria* had long passed, *Adrenalize* was out for some time, and "newbie" Vivian Campbell was in the early days of his time with the band.

It was a captivating moment in time to witness with my newfound perspective, and frankly, also frustrating at times, especially when observing the challenges Def Leppard was up against, in particular having to cope with an ever-growing grunge movement and a music industry that was becoming increasingly less favorable to the band.

Def Leppard was no longer ruling the charts consistently as they did in years past; radio stations were changing formats to accommodate shifting listener tastes and were nowhere near as welcoming when it came to playing the band's latest single, and mainstream music tastes were moving further and further away from Def Leppard's brand of music.

Did that stop Def Leppard? Absolutely not. Witnessing the band remain intensely devoted to doing whatever they could to help promote their music to the masses, and continuously give a hundred percent to cater to their dedicated fan base is something I will always remember.

A primary reason why I launched a Def Leppard-centric fan website (DefLeppardReport.com aka "The Lep Report") was because of my fond experiences meeting fans over those years, and hearing about how much they admired the band and just couldn't get enough. Whether they were attending their first, fiftieth, or hundredth Def Leppard show -- it didn't really matter -- the exhilaration felt by all of them was mutual.

The same applies to fans of other bands I had the opportunity to work with. It was always gratifying to be a part of, or at least help contribute to, making their dreams come true.

One example was during Bon Jovi's *These Days* tour. Having the seat information for a list of contest winners, I helped out by going into the venue's seating area mid-show to locate and inform them that it was their turn to go up on stage and watch the band perform. (There was a bar-like setting at the side of the stage; several groups of winners got to sit at the "bar" to watch Bon Jovi perform select songs close up.) It was quite a workout tracking these fans down in a darkened venue with music blaring and concert lights beaming, escorting them through the rowdy crowd to the backstage area, and then doing it all over again with the next group of winners. But it was a joy seeing the excited looks on all their faces before and after the experience.

Another example is KISS and the band's very passionate fan base. Being involved in a local radio promotion for a select group of contest winners to not only have the opportunity to meet their music idols but also sit down and eat lunch with the band is another stand-out memory. (Partaking in the lunch myself, and being a big glam rock fan, I found it most enjoyable discussing Mott The Hoople with KISS drummer Eric Singer.)

On a related note, I had the unique opportunity to ride in a limousine with KISS in 1993, as we traveled from the downtown Chicago hotel the band was staying at to a private, autograph signing event that had been set up for fans at a venue called Medusa's. (The purpose of the event was to promote the band's upcoming *Alive III* release.)

Ironically, my childhood memories of KISS -- aside from being a pop culture phenomenon -- mainly centered around, um ... how do I put it ... fear! I wasn't even 10 years old when I first saw Gene Simmons in his "Demon" character make-up, spitting out blood while watching him on TV in the late '70s. Observing that spectacle scared the bejesus out of me, literally causing me nightmares as a kid. Having the opportunity decades later to work with KISS directly was something I never *ever* would have imagined, and something I will never forget.

One quick tidbit: I was told by a coworker when getting ready to work my first KISS-involved project that "Gene could be intimidating," not necessarily in his one-of-a-kind demeanor but just in his imposing appearance, particularly his height. I didn't think much about it at first, but decided to prepare myself as best I could for the initial encounter: I made sure to wear my oh-so-stylish '90s "shoe-boots" which had heels that somewhat enhanced my six-foot frame. It didn't matter, though, as Gene showed up wearing a pair of boots of his own with heels -- no, not his KISS platform boots, as this was during KISS's non-makeup era, but boots nonetheless, which added additional inches to his height. Regardless, I was able to face my childhood fears head-on with the man behind that indelible Demon stage persona. My interactions with him were...memorable, but that's a whole other story!

These are just some of the *other* unforgettable memories that ensued along the way of my unique journey.

So come on along and let's revisit more of them, specifically the ones involving Def Leppard because *I Got Something To Say!*, and I wanted to share some of my personal, first-hand experiences and behind-the-scenes stories with you -- recollections and reflections never written about before -- along with several other inside peeks and never-before-seen pictures from my Def Leppard vault.

This is all in addition to the main crux of this book, which features in-depth write-ups of each of the band's original studio albums (plus *Retro Active*) as well as select single releases. There is also a chapter dedicated to Steve Clark, as well as one dissecting Mutt Lange's undeniable impact and body of work. While some of these in-depth album and single write-ups were originally posted on DefLeppardReport.com, they all have been completely refreshed from beginning to end. The chapters spotlighting these releases not only include analysis of things like chart performance but also revisits (caution: sometimes with a very critical eye!) the marketing and promotional strategies used to promote them.

Lastly, when I first launched The Lep Report website, I decided to kick things off with what seemed like a fun yet challenging and thought-provoking exercise: ranking and reviewing the songs from each Def Leppard original studio album. The mini-review for each song has been thoroughly refreshed for this book.

Thanks for being here. Sit back, relax, and get ready to indulge in some Def Leppard. Okay, *a lot* of Def Leppard!

Hope you enjoy the ride.

Personal Story: Stumping Sav

One of my favorite moments the day of a Def Leppard show did *not* occur during a pre-show event or meet and greet, or even during the concert itself. (Though to be clear, all the personal recollections included in this book are memorable in their own right!)

What always felt extra special to me was the "after-show." No, I'm not referring to wild, chaotic partying. Actually, it was quite the opposite: the anticipation that had been building up to the concert had subsided, adrenaline levels were returning to normal, and now there was a more relaxed atmosphere for everybody to cool down, decompress, and celebrate the evening's event.

This was rather contrary to how I perceived and experienced things in prior years (i.e., before working at the band's record label), specifically as a fan attending a Def Leppard show.

Back then, the concert was the evening's main attraction, and as enjoyable as it was, all the way up to the encore's final song, there was also a sense of sadness knowing the experience was just about over. Soon enough, like a cold splash of reality, the venue's house lights would inevitably turn on and remind you that the ride had come to an end and that it was time to go home.

I'm sure you can relate: you're on a concert high and you don't want the night to end, or at the least, wish it would go on for a little while longer. Come on, one more song! But, alas, all good things come to an end when the venue's curfew strikes!

But that wasn't the case during my time in the music business, which made me appreciate the opportunities presented all the more.

So back to one particular moment I wanted to share with you.

Def Leppard's concert was over. The band had a chance to cool down, change into some comfortable clothes, and just...chill out.

A private hotel suite/bar would be reserved and set up where the band, friends, record company personnel, and others such as program directors and other reps from local radio stations that (usually) supported the band's music, were invited to attend and hang out.

It was very casual and mellow -- you could serve yourself at the stocked bar if there wasn't a bartender around (I was never much of a drinker, but the ginger ale was fantastic), have a seat and chat with others in the room, usually about the evening's concert highlights.

At some point, band members would arrive and join the festivities.

While hanging out at the hotel bar area after the show and chatting with others, in walks Sav, grabbing a bottle of his drink of choice and pouring himself a glass.

During this time, I had been talking to a local radio program director in the region (Indianapolis), and we were engaged in a fun little game of Def Leppard *Hysteria* album trivia.

A quick aside: being a passionate Def Leppard fan, I always took great pride in knowing as much information as possible about the band -- this applied even before I worked at the band's label, but I considered it even more important -- a duty, if you will -- to stay on top of things while I was there. Read the latest magazine interview and what it entailed? Check. Know the latest album and single sales and chart data? Check. And so on. If there was any tidbit of information, no matter how small, I would do my best to know about it.

That being said, after some back and forth of trying to challenge and one-up each other during our trivia competition, one of my questions bewildered the program director. So we ended up calling out to Sav and pulled him into the discussion, asking if he could answer it. Who better to ask?!

Sav was game. Ready and willing to take it on.

My question to him: "There seems to be a mistake in the liner notes of the *Hysteria* album. A word is repeated twice in the long list you guys wrote describing engineer Nigel Green. What is that word?"

I will never forget Sav's hilarious reaction: an exasperated look on his face immediately followed by "Oh, fook!" (I've spelled the word phonetically.)

We all enjoyed a laugh at his response, and after about ten seconds of Sav deep in thought, repeating the question to himself, and thinking it over, he eventually responded with: "I dunno. What is it?"

Now, allow me to pause ever so briefly from continuing this story to properly let this unique moment sink in. As a Def Leppard fan, put yourself in my place: the surrealness of hanging out after the concert, having drinks with Sav, and not only that, stumping *him* on Def Leppard -- better yet, *Hysteria* -- trivia!

I certainly have to cut Sav some slack, though. After a long day of promotional appearances and events, performing for thousands of fans earlier in the evening, and just wanting to unwind and enjoy a drink, I have no doubt his mindset wasn't in the best place to answer an inconsequential trivia question.

Personally, while I was amused that I caught the repeated word when I noticed it in *Hysteria*'s liner notes years prior, I *never* thought I'd actually be asking one of Def Leppard's members about it. Who knows, maybe Joe, walking music encyclopedia that he is, would have known the answer. Maybe not. Not that it matters. But Sav was the first one from the band to arrive in the room that evening, so he was the chosen one.

So, you might be wondering right about now: What the heck was the word?

Well, in case you weren't already aware or caught it yourself, the word is...*mole*, which I finally divulged to Sav.

And here's something really neat which further made this moment memorable: After telling Sav the answer, he went on to explain why the term was even used as a descriptor. ("Oh, yeah! The reason we called him that was because...") To paraphrase Sav's answer to me, Nigel was behind the recording studio glass, at the mixing console, and the band would frequently see his head pop up every so often, like a mole, or as I interpreted Sav's explanation, in a "whack-a-mole"-type way.

As a fan, it was a real treat to get the additional context as to why the word was used in the first place, not to mention learning about it directly from Sav. It's definitely not something I would have figured out doing my own research!

I jokingly take pride in "stumping Sav" but I genuinely do appreciate the moment and discovering yet another interesting, albeit obscure, detail about the *Hysteria* album. That's what makes it all the more special.

Regardless of whether the word *mole* was repeated or not -- which by the way it *still* is, even in the reprint of the *Hysteria* Deluxe Edition -- it's fun to reminisce about.

After getting Sav's explanation that day, it was gratifying to tell other Def Leppard fans about the repeated word *and* its intended meaning. And when asked how I knew, proudly responding with "Sav told me!"

Personal Story: A Special Radio Request

Sometimes it's the little things that count.

I always found it amusing traveling to a town where Def Leppard would be performing later that evening and hearing local rock stations promote the event.

Having just gone through similar concert hysteria (pun intended) in a previous city, it would still be just as exciting to re-experience that same pre-show anticipation with a whole new audience on a different night.

On some occasions, the record label's regional radio promotion rep and I would be driving to a local radio station to pick up the program director (or music director, DJ, etc.) who would be attending the Def Leppard festivities (concert, meet and greet, etc.) that evening.

This also provided the opportunity to meet face-to-face and discuss other (i.e., non-Def Leppard) releases with them. "There's a new Bon Jovi track you have to check out, and a new Scorpions album coming out in a couple of months your listeners will love. Take a listen..."

Basically, schmoozing and making the most of the time. A productive mix of work and leisure.

There were times we would contact a radio station rep on our way to pick them up or, in some cases, even if they weren't attending the evening's events, and the label rep I was with would mention to the radio contact on the phone, *"I've got a huge Def Leppard fan here with me"* as he would be discussing the band and subtly going over selling points, *"and he says their next single is going to be a big hit!"* In other words, using some good-natured humor and sarcasm to make a persuasive Def Leppard pitch to them. Might as well make the "job" more fun if you have to do it!

On the other end of the telephone line, the radio station contact would usually be entertained by the pitch and, at times, be kind enough to respond with something along the lines of, *"We'll play something for him on the air...What Def Leppard song does he want to hear?"* What a cool gesture!

This occurred during the *Adrenalize/Retro Active* era, so it wouldn't have been out of the ordinary for my "radio request" to be a more recent hit like "Let's Get Rocked," or maybe the popular ballad "Two Steps Behind," or simply go with one of Def Leppard's radio classics like "Photograph" or "Pour Some Sugar On Me."

But I would never go with any of those song choices because they were too predictable -- the station would likely play one of them at some point anyway.

I much preferred to go a different route. And what better way to do that than have the city's rock station shock some of its listeners by playing..."Gods of War." That's right, my selection would be the 6-minute, 30-second-plus Def Leppard deep track epic they would never play otherwise.

Additionally, I considered it a nice, subtle tribute to Steve Clark, who had passed away just several years prior. Plus, any Def Leppard fans listening would be pleasantly surprised with the rare occurrence of the track played on their radio station.

Within 15 minutes or so after making the special request, and still in the car with the radio blaring while driving to the evening's concert, the unmistakable opening of "Gods of War" would begin...as would the smile on my face.

"Feelin' like it's over...."

A perfect set-up to an evening of Def Leppard festivities!

If by chance any Def Leppard fans in the Midwest recall hearing, or being baffled by, "Gods of War" played on their local rock radio station the night of their town's Def Leppard concert in the mid-'90s, well...you're welcome. (Ha!)

Album Spotlight: *On Through The Night*

Def Leppard's debut album *On Through The Night* was released in March 1980 and remains a rather polarizing release to this day.

Some very passionate fans adamantly consider it to be the best album the band ever recorded, with every subsequent Def Leppard album release -- including *Pyromania* and *Hysteria* -- paling in comparison.

Other fans vehemently beg to differ. They believe *On Through The Night* is Def Leppard's weakest release, a respectable effort that showcases the talents of an up-and-coming band, one that will require a couple more albums to mature and master its craft (with the help of Mutt Lange) to reach its true potential.

The band themselves have gone on the record (excuse the pun) saying they don't consider *On Through The Night* anywhere near their greatest effort. This should come as no surprise, as tracks from the album rarely appear on Def Leppard's concert setlists.

Here's how Joe Elliott described *On Through The Night* in an interview with AVClub.com:

> "You know, a lot of people got a great affection for that record, but as I always say, 'Yeah, but it's hardly the first Van Halen or Boston album, is it?'

"The one good thing about it was it gave us a launchpad to get better from. And I believe that when we got to High 'n' Dry and on to Pyromania and Hysteria, we started doing the record the first album should have been... It was fun working with Tom [Allom, producer], but we spent most of the time drinking wine and having a good time as opposed to making a good record... It's a bit naive and it could have been a better record."

Love it or hate it, *On Through The Night* is a piece of the fabric that ultimately made Def Leppard the band it is today. It's also one of *only* four albums guitarist Steve Clark performed on, yet another reason why many fans still look back on it so fondly.

Album Sales Performance

On Through The Night's sales are nowhere near Def Leppard's biggest albums, selling "only" one million copies, a number that was bolstered by *Pyromania* and *Hysteria*, monster-selling releases which inevitably brought newfound consumer attention to the band's early catalog.

During its original chart run, *On Through The Night* peaked at #51 on *Billboard*'s top albums chart, which is respectable for a debut album, especially one from a band that didn't have much notoriety at the time.

The week *On Through The Night* peaked, *Billboard*'s album chart was ruled by Billy Joel (*Glass Houses*), Eric Clapton (*Just One Night*), Paul McCartney (*McCartney II*), Bob Seger & The Silver Bullet Band (*Against The Wind*), and *The Empire Strikes Back* soundtrack -- a somewhat eclectic mix.

But further down the chart, it's worth noting that some of the other albums were from music acts that included Van

Halen, Journey, Black Sabbath, Ted Nugent, Judas Priest, Alice Cooper, KISS, Scorpions, and Sammy Hagar. Thus, Def Leppard was entering a fairly welcoming environment (music-wise *and* touring-wise) as they began to make their mark in the United States.

Watch Out For The Rock Brigade

Regardless of your Def Leppard album preference, *On Through The Night* includes some genuinely solid hard-rock tracks. Most notably, "Wasted" (and its unmistakable riff), "Rock Brigade," and "It Don't Matter." They all still pack a wallop.

Fittingly, the album's 40th anniversary was commemorated as part of the band's *The Early Years* box set release, which also included a remastered version of the *High 'n' Dry* album, and numerous other extras -- B-sides, rarities and re-mix versions, *Radio One* sessions, Live from Reading, and the first-ever appearance of an unreleased and newly mixed show from Oxford in 1980 -- offering fans new and old the opportunity to revisit and rediscover Def Leppard's earliest era.

And who can forget "Hello America," a song which, true to its title, introduced the band to American audiences.

Joe Elliott discussed the song's origins with Rolling Stone:

> "We had never even been to America at that point. I was working in a factory with lots of nuts and bolts and no natural light. But there was a lot of downtime, and I would sit around writing stuff. With this one, I had seen a TV show the night before — 'Kojak' or 'Starsky & Hutch,' something where they show the tree-lined boulevards of L.A. You see all these palm trees and you go, 'Wow, this is a lot sexier than Sheffield!' That's where that lyric came from — 'Well I'm takin' me a trip/I'm

going down to Californ-i-a. It was, 'Get me out of here!'"

Since that time, Def Leppard assembled a deep catalog filled with iconic songs, became a Rock & Roll Hall of Fame inductee, remains an in-demand touring attraction, and still releases new music on occasion.

Unquestionably, the band has come a *long* way.

What is also undeniable is that *On Through The Night* played a key role in laying the runway for their extraordinary journey to take flight, and putting Def Leppard on a path to achieve many remarkable milestones throughout its illustrious career.

The band may not have realized it back in 1980 with *On Through The Night*'s release, but their rock brigade was only just beginning.

Album Spotlight: *High 'n' Dry*

Def Leppard's *High 'n' Dry* album was released in July 1981.

It may be easy for some to overlook the significance of Def Leppard's second studio album, with the band's subsequent, incredibly successful follow-ups *Pyromania* and *Hysteria* overshadowing it. Yet there is a sizable group of Def Leppard fans who maintain that the *High 'n' Dry* album not only is the band's best release but the band *at its best* -- from its songs, sound, and attitude to the band member line-up.

Regardless of the band era you favor, *High 'n' Dry* is arguably Def Leppard's most important album.

If debut album *On Through The Night* planted the proverbial seeds of a young band's budding talents, *High 'n' Dry* saw those seeds break ground and begin to bloom, revealing what Def Leppard was truly capable of.

A New High

High 'n' Dry showcased a more finely crafted version of Def Leppard. Whereas *On Through The Night* introduced the band's ability to rock hard, *High 'n' Dry* confirmed it wasn't a fluke by repeating the same feat, just on a much grander scale.

High 'n' Dry charted a course that would reward the band with spectacular success(es) for decades to come. Uncoincidentally, *High 'n' Dry* was also the first time Def Leppard collaborated with record producer extraordinaire Robert John "Mutt" Lange, who brought out the best in the band as only he could: Joe Elliott's thick vocals sounded more powerful and confident, guitar portions were more ambitious and tighter in their arrangements, bass and drums were more substantial and prominent in keeping the tempo.

The album's production exhibited a raw, hard edge throughout. And while sleeker than *On Through The Night*, it would still sound less polished and not as multi-layered compared to the band's future album releases.

Ultimately, *High 'n' Dry* struck the right balance, engulfing listeners with its distinct hard rock sound, all the while infusing each of its songs with an ample amount of Def Leppard's (and Mutt Lange's) melodic sensibilities.

A Seventh Band Member?

It's been said numerous times over the years that producer Mutt Lange is Def Leppard's unofficial sixth band member. Here's another Def Leppard hyperbole: In addition to Mutt Lange, *High 'n' Dry* features a seventh member...in the form of guitars.

The album showcases Def Leppard's guitar sound in a way that's unlike any of the band's other albums, courtesy of the masterful dual assault from guitarists Steve Clark and Pete Willis.

Revisit the *High 'n' Dry* album and pay extra attention to the guitar parts throughout all the songs -- not just the guitar solos (or "Switch 625") -- and listen to how the guitars complement and interact with Joe Elliott's vocals. They are so prevalent and practically have a voice of their own.

Mutt Lange's influence and involvement certainly played a part in the accomplishment, but the majority of the credit goes to Steve Clark and Pete Willis, two of *High 'n' Dry*'s most integral contributors.

High 'n' Dry Is Not About The Singles

Even though *High 'n' Dry* left an indelible mark, the album surprisingly does not contain any singles that were major hits.

The album did have *some* radio support: "Let It Go" (originally titled "When The Rain Falls") did receive decent radio play and ended up charting, peaking at #34 on *Billboard*'s less consequential, more niche Mainstream Rock chart.

Sentimental favorite "Bringin' On the Heartbreak" (originally titled "A Certain Heartache") was also a single, but it didn't do much chart-wise. It wasn't until three years later, due to the success of *Pyromania*, that "Bringin' On the Heartbreak" was remixed, revived, and re-released as a single (with B-side "Me and My Wine").

Timing-wise, it all worked out splendidly and to the band's advantage, due mostly in part to the support of up-and-coming cable network MTV.

Not only did the remixed version's music video feature an entertaining, albeit overly dramatic, storyline when compared to the original single's video (which featured a straightforward concert performance), but it also provided the band with the opportunity to feature Pete Willis' replacement, new guitarist Phil Collen. (Coincidentally, Pete Willis was fired from Def Leppard exactly one year to the day of *High 'n' Dry*'s U.S. release.)

In the end, the "Bringin' On the Heartbreak" re-release peaked at #61 on *Billboard*'s Hot 100 singles chart and helped introduce the band to international audiences. But it wouldn't be until *Pyromania* that they would discover the true meaning of commercial success.

Another *High 'n' Dry* Album? Let It Go!

While *High 'n' Dry* remains *the* go-to album for numerous Def Leppard fans, some still long for the band to revisit the same hard rock sound that made the album such an unforgettable favorite.

There have been moments since its release when a Def Leppard song has arguably captured *High 'n' Dry*'s harder vibe: "Four Letter Word," "Forever Young," and "Broke 'N' Brokenhearted" are just a few recent examples.

With that said, could Def Leppard realistically record another album that resembles *High 'n' Dry*? No, for three very important reasons.

First, it's not the type of album (i.e., music) the band is particularly interested in recording at this stage of their career.

Second, without Mutt Lange's involvement, the project becomes even further out of reach.

Third, the band no longer includes the two band members who were essential in creating *High 'n' Dry*: Steve Clark and Pete Willis.

Aside from all the brilliant guitar licks, riffs, and shredding solos each contributed throughout the album, Steve and Pete also co-wrote *nearly every song* on *High 'n' Dry*. (Interestingly, two additional song gems from the *High 'n' Dry* recording sessions were left unfinished, becoming a part of *Pyromania* instead: "Rock! Rock! (Till You Drop)" and "Photograph.")

Here is a breakdown of the *High 'n' Dry* album's tracklisting, along with who wrote each song (bold emphasis added to illustrate the point):

- "Let It Go" (Writers: **Pete Willis**, **Steve Clark**, Joe Elliott)
- "Another Hit and Run" (Writers: Rick Savage, Joe Elliott)
- "High 'n' Dry (Saturday Night)" (Writers: **Steve Clark**, Rick Savage Joe Elliott)

- "Bringin' On the Heartbreak" (Writers: **Steve Clark**, **Pete Willis**, Joe Elliott)
- "Switch 625" (Writer: **Steve Clark**)
- "You Got Me Runnin'" (Writers: **Pete Willis**, **Steve Clark**, Joe Elliott)
- "Lady Strange" (Writers: **Pete Willis**, **Steve Clark**, Rick Allen, Joe Elliott)
- "On Through the Night" (Writers: **Steve Clark**, Rick Savage, Joe Elliott)
- "Mirror, Mirror (Look into My Eyes)" (Writers: **Steve Clark**, Joe Elliott)
- "No No No" (Writers: Rick Savage, **Pete Willis**, Joe Elliott)

Bottom line: Revisiting the magic created during the band's *High 'n' Dry* era isn't possible, especially without the input and immense contributions of original members Steve Clark and Pete Willis.

So, best to savor the album for what it is and was, and leave it at that.

High 'n' Dry To This Day

The band still includes some *High 'n' Dry* representation on tour.

"Bringin' On the Heartbreak" (the only track off the album that's included on the band's first greatest hits release, *Vault*) is usually a given, and songs like "Let It Go," "Another Hit and Run," and "High 'n' Dry (Saturday Night)" have occasionally made it onto setlists, too.

Even "Switch 625" became a setlist staple for some time, though performing Steve Clark's epic opus without Steve himself just isn't quite the same.

The *High 'n' Dry* Album Experience

High 'n' Dry wasn't a monster-selling album like *Pyromania* and *Hysteria*. It peaked at #38 on *Billboard*'s top albums chart and ended up reaching double platinum, a far cry from the albums that would follow it.

Yet make no mistake, it paved the way.

High 'n' Dry is also structurally unique in how it deviates from the likes of *Pyromania* and *Hysteria*. For example, three songs can easily be selected off of *Hysteria* (let's say "Pour Some Sugar on Me," "Animal," and "Hysteria") as well as *Pyromania* ("Photograph," "Rock of Ages," and "Foolin'") to sum up or best represent those respective albums.

High 'n' Dry is a different animal.

Even though all of *High 'n' Dry*'s songs can stand on their own, the best way to truly appreciate their unrelenting intensity is to listen to the entire album all the way through. That's how well they all flow into each other. It's a prime example where the whole is far greater and even more impressive than the sum of its parts. Thus, choosing only a handful of select songs (or singles) would be too limiting and do the album a disservice.

An Impressive Hit (And Run)

Commercial success or not, *High 'n' Dry* laid the groundwork for the band to build upon going forward. It also marked the beginning of a career-changing collaboration: Def Leppard working with Mutt Lange.

Without *High 'n' Dry* and the opportunity to work with Mutt, there likely never would have been a *Pyromania* or *Hysteria*, or at the very least, the type of albums they ended up being.

Fortunately, we'll never know, but that's how significant and vital *High 'n' Dry* was in directing Def Leppard's career path to superstardom.

Final Thoughts

High 'n' Dry is an excellent sophomore effort, to put it mildly. Not only is it a classic, but it's also in a class by itself. It's a transformative album, one that was pivotal in defining who Def Leppard was, and authoritatively positioned the band for what it could (and would) ultimately become.

In a 1981 *Rockline* interview, a young Joe Elliott humbly explained what the band tried to achieve with the *High 'n' Dry* album:

> "We're just trying to get energy across really, that's all. We just like playing rock 'n' roll. That's the music we've grown up on, that's the music we'll always play. And we're just an energetic band live, and we try to get it across on record..."

The band unequivocally accomplished that and so much more. And even though more commercially successful Def Leppard albums would follow it, High 'n' Dry's impact still resonates powerfully to this day.

Album Spotlight: *Pyromania*

Pyromania was released in January 1983.

On Through The Night and *High 'n' Dry* could be considered the appetizers to Def Leppard's *Pyromania,* the main course of finely crafted songs that would propel the band toward superstardom. (It wouldn't be until 4 years later when a heaping second helping -- the *Hysteria* album -- would lift them to even greater heights.)

Fans are passionate about which Def Leppard era or album best represents the band, but, regardless of choice, it's undeniable that *Pyromania* was groundbreaking.

So rise up, gather round -- better yet, sit back and get comfortable -- and let's rock this deep dive to the ground by taking a fond look back at Def Leppard's iconic *Pyromania* album.

Pete Willis: F-F-F-Fired

Though it may sound cliché, the *Pyromania* period was indeed a time of transition for Def Leppard. (In the '80s and '90s, this seemed to be more the norm than the exception for the band.)

Founding member Pete Willis was fired during the recording of the album. And while his rhythm guitar work remained on the record, *Pyromania* ended up being the first Def Leppard album to feature Phil Collen, Willis' replacement.

Pete Willis was a key part in co-writing numerous songs during the band's early era, including the *Pyromania* album: "Photograph," "Too Late For Love," "Comin' Under Fire," and "Billy's Got A Gun" were all co-written by him.

It's important to note that Steve Clark's songwriting contributions were also all over the album. Aside from "Stagefright," Steve co-wrote every song on *Pyromania*. (Phil Collen joined the band near the end of the album's recording; he was not involved in co-writing any of the tracks.)

Together, Steve Clark and Pete Willis played a crucial part in making the band's first three studio albums, well, what they were. And *Pyromania* marked the end of that creative force.

Teaming up Steve and Phil -- aka "The Terror Twins" -- introduced a whole new dynamic. And while Phil did not take part in the songwriting process, he delivered unmistakable guitar solos on five of *Pyromania's* songs -- "Photograph" being one of them -- while Steve handled solos on the album's five other tracks.

Mutt Lange's Return & Influence

Producer Robert John "Mutt" Lange took on a much greater role in crafting *Pyromania*, and, ultimately, the type of band Def Leppard would become.

Mutt's involvement in the album went far beyond producer duties; for instance, aside from Joe Elliott, Mutt is the only other person to have a songwriting credit on every *Pyromania* track.

It was during this time Def Leppard's rough-around-the-edges, hard rock sound began to transform. With Mutt's influential direction, the band that had put out *On Through The Night* and *High 'n' Dry* was now evolving into a more polished, arena-rocking, radio-friendly, rock supergroup.

Joe Elliott addressed why Def Leppard's sound drastically changed after *High 'n' Dry* in an interview with *Rolling Stone*, mentioning:

> "We never wanted to be the band that set up and played, which is what we were for High 'n' Dry – and that's what we wanted to be for High 'n' Dry because there was no technology then."

In hindsight, *Pyromania* bridged the gap between the band's first two "rawer" studio albums and subsequent multi-layered productions like *Hysteria*, *Adrenalize*, and beyond (such as *Euphoria*).

And while some fans may have been disappointed by Def Leppard's more refined "commercial" sound during the *Pyromania* (and *Hysteria*) era, it's that particular sound that ultimately became the band's trademark and an essential ingredient to its success and enduring popularity.

No Serenade, No Fire Brigade, Just *Pyromania*

Pyromania packs a wallop, from the opening jolt of "Rock! Rock! (Till You Drop)" to the seemingly endless drum loops that follow final track "Billy's Got A Gun."

The album ventures into different directions -- many tracks even feature distinct sound effects to announce (and identify) them before any music actually begins -- all of which contribute to *Pyromania's* unique listening experience.

When a young, talented band works with a mastermind producer, magical results are sure to ensue, and the differences on *Pyromania* are stark when compared to previous Def Leppard albums: Joe Elliott's vocals are much more controlled and powerful; Steve Clark and Phil Collen's (and Pete Willis') guitars are crisp and impactful; Rick Savage's bass guitar is prominent and ever-present as it leads the way; the layered backing vocals (which also include Mutt Lange's voice) are thunderous.

And then there were the drums, an essential component in what made *Pyromania's* songs -- and the album's almighty sound -- so distinct.

What may be surprising to some is that the majority of the drums heard on *Pyromania* (aside from cymbals and other fills throughout) were reportedly created by drum machines -- a trade-off to accomplish the sound Mutt Lange envisioned for the album, and the result of his recording approach (i.e., adding drum tracks last for more flexibility when arranging and rearranging songs).

Mutt Lange's right-hand man and engineer-extraordinaire, the late Mike Shipley confirmed this recording process in interviews:

> *"Take 'Photograph,' for example. Like all the other songs on the record, the song's drums were all samples from the Fairlight [CMI (computer musical instrument) sampler]. There are no real drums. The cymbals are played, but the bass drum, snare, and toms are all machine."*

Ironically, this all occurred *before* Rick Allen's tragic car accident, which resulted in him completely changing his approach to drumming, and, subsequently, further transforming Def Leppard's sound.

As for *Pyromania*, it was Mutt Lange's overall approach and attention to detail that ended up creating such a tremendous-sounding outcome.

Pyromania's Singles And Beyond

Pyromania's official singles lit up the charts, yet none of them came close to topping *Billboard*'s Hot 100 singles chart; surprisingly, they didn't even reach the Top 10. That's not to say they didn't make an impact; they certainly did, leaving a lasting impression to this day.

"Photograph," which many consider the album's best track, was the first official single -- talk about an excellent way to introduce *Pyromania* to a radio audience! The song peaked at #12 on *Billboard*'s Hot 100 singles chart (it reached #1 on the more niche Mainstream Rock chart).

Surprisingly, and indicative of Def Leppard's long uphill climb to win over audiences in their homeland, "Photograph" peaked at only #66 on the U.K.'s singles chart.

"Rock of Ages" followed it up as the album's second single in May 1983, nearly matching "Photograph's" chart performance. It reached #16 on the Hot 100 singles chart (and also made it to #1 on the Mainstream Rock chart).

"Foolin'" was released (in North America only) as single number three in November 1983, and didn't quite keep up with its predecessors, peaking at #28 on the Hot 100 singles chart (and #9 on the Mainstream Rock chart).

And then...that was it.

You may be wondering, what about "Too Late for Love"? The song was never officially released as a single in North America. (It was a single in the U.K., peaking at #86.)

The point in all of this is not to provide a Def Leppard chart lesson, but to show that *Pyromania* succeeded *in spite of* not having many singles, let alone ones that conquered the charts.

In the span of 7 months, all of the album's singles had come and gone. There was no second wave of radio-friendly releases, no additional singles timed with another leg of the *Pyromania* tour, etc. Fini!

Quite a few of *Pyromania's* powerhouse deep tracks (such as "Too Late for Love," "Comin' Under Fire," and "Billy's Got A Gun") still made it onto the Mainstream Rock chart, though, to help keep the album's momentum going. In the process, these classic "non-singles" also made a name for themselves.

Overall, this was a more successful, tactical approach than, say, the single release strategies for *X* and *Adrenalize*. (See the write-ups for those albums for more about that topic.)

The band also made great use of the album's deep cuts on tour, well beyond the *Pyromania* era: "Stagefright" and "Rock! Rock! (Till You Drop)" were effectively utilized as opening numbers during the *Hysteria* tour. "Too Late For Love," "Die Hard The Hunter," and "Billy's Got A Gun" remain concert highlights and were even performed during 2019's "Hits Vegas" residency. (It goes to show the caliber of *Pyromania's* songs; any of the tracks mentioned above, though not technically singles or hits, could easily fit into a Def Leppard setlist even now.)

As for the album's official singles, one major reason their popularity soared initially was due to the support of up-and-coming cable network MTV. Back then, viewers rarely made it through a day without seeing Def Leppard appear on the channel, be it an interview or the heavy rotation of the "Photograph," "Rock of Ages," and "Foolin'" music videos.

The album's marketing strategy was straightforward yet significant and also helped enhance Def Leppard's brand: By the end of *Pyromania's* promotional run, people undoubtedly knew who Def Leppard was, and they were well aware of the band's sound and image (which included the often-seen, emblematic Union Jack flag). Furthermore, the band was successfully positioned as a rock music force to be reckoned with.

Pyromania provided Def Leppard with the opportunity to finally hit it big -- really big -- in North America, and the band took full advantage of it. Merely two years prior to the album's release, Def Leppard was opening for music acts such as Rainbow, Judas Priest, and Ozzy Osbourne; as a result of *Pyromania's* success, the band was able to headline their very own tour, which they did for nearly 200 dates.

Sizzling Sales

Pyromania was a huge seller for Def Leppard, even though Michael Jackson's *Thriller* (and the *Flashdance* soundtrack) prevented it from reaching #1 on *Billboard*'s top albums chart.

Regardless, the album achieved its goal of helping Def Leppard cross over and conquer American music audiences. (It would take years for the band to accomplish the same feat in the U.K., where *Pyromania* didn't even reach the Top 10, peaking at #18.)

The album ultimately reached diamond certification status (over 10 million copies sold) in the U.S. alone.

Final Thoughts

Pyromania may have only been Def Leppard's third studio album, but nearly four decades after its release, it's still considered one of the band's greatest accomplishments.

The album's classic tracks remain iconic and evergreen; it wouldn't be an overstatement to say a song like "Photograph" could *still* be a hit today.

This is all due to the strength and unwavering quality of *Pyromania*. It emphatically set its own standard, a big reason why it remains incredibly resilient.

The same can be said of Def Leppard.

Still rollin', rock 'n' rollin'...

Album Spotlight: *Hysteria*

Def Leppard's *Hysteria* album was released in August 1987.

There's much to celebrate about the band's landmark album, including its meticulous production, seemingly endless amount of hit songs, incredible chart longevity, and extraordinary sales performance.

But, wait, there's more!

If you have already read some of the other "album spotlight" chapters in this book, you're likely aware of some of the dissections written about Def Leppard's original studio albums. But this time around, a slightly different approach will be taken.

This will still most definitely be a *very* deep dive, but to properly commemorate *Hysteria* and truly appreciate the release for what it is, it's important to also recognize the album for what it's *not* (but easily could have been).

Hysteria Memories

Hysteria is a prime example of how even when so many things go wrong, the final result can still be oh so right.

The challenges and detours that delayed making the *Hysteria* album, including the unimaginable tragedy of drummer Rick Allen losing his arm (and nearly his life) in a car accident, reinforces the old adage that "everything happens for a reason."

Def Leppard's *Hysteria* is not only iconic and by far the band's most commercially successful release, but it's also one of the top-selling albums of *all time* -- not all that surprising, considering it's arguably a greatest hits compilation in and of itself.

Decades after its release, the album remains a favorite among many fans -- no Def Leppard tour would be complete without a healthy dose of *Hysteria* representation; fans demand it, the band knows it and obliges.

Hysteria helped define music in the late '80s; it was nearly impossible to get through a day without hearing a song off the album on the radio or seeing one of its music videos on MTV.

It's an album ingrained in the youth of countless fans, and part of so many cherished memories, making repeated listens all the more nostalgic, joyful, and satisfying. From opening track "Women" to its final song "Love and Affection," an adventurous, unforgettable sixty-two-minute-plus music journey always awaits.

By the summer of 1988, Def Leppard had become one of the biggest bands in the world, predominantly due to what they accomplished with *Hysteria*. It's not a coincidence that the album's massive world tour lasted *years*.

Animal Instinct...When You're Near?

Simply saying the word "Hysteria" immediately brings to mind a certain feeling, mood, or memory for many Def Leppard fans, a testament to its impact and how much the album still resonates.

Hysteria worked so well as an album title, too. Besides representing what the band had to endure during the album's prolonged recording process (particularly Rick Allen after his car accident), it was yet another single-word title ending in "ia," serendipitously linking it to the band's previous album *Pyromania*, which was also one word and ended in "ia."

It's difficult to imagine referring to the album by its original working title, *Animal Instinct*. While the phrase may work splendidly as a lyric in the song "Women" -- *"The animal instinct, the wanton man"* -- it just doesn't have the same pay-off when representing the album as a whole. (It's worth noting David Fricke's excellent late-'80s Def Leppard book did retain the *Animal Instinct* title.)

Hysteria: The Singles

Numerous singles contributed to making *Hysteria* so memorable, including one that was a complete misfire.

The album's first U.S. single "Women" tanked badly. (The band wanted "Animal" to launch the album, but their management at the time disagreed.) The single *barely* made it onto *Billboard*'s Hot 100 singles chart, peaking at #80 and hampering *Hysteria*'s initial album sales in the process.

It wasn't until second single "Animal" was released that *some* album sales momentum returned, as the song narrowly cracked the Top 20 on Billboard's singles chart.

This led the way to title track "Hysteria," the album's third single and first bonafide hit, as it reached the Top 10 on *Billboard*'s Hot 100 chart.

Now let's take a moment to revisit what did *not* become Def Leppard's fourth studio album.

Hysteria: An Alternative Take

Early on, Def Leppard's fourth album didn't sound anything like *Hysteria*. It was more along the lines of *Retro Active*.

The reason being, quite a few songs that ended up on *Retro*

Active were actually songs that were originally recorded for the band's fourth release.

If things had worked out differently, this write-up would be discussing songs such as "I Wanna Be Your Hero" and "Ring of Fire," potentially as well as tracks that were left unfinished (after the album project completely changed direction) like "Desert Song" and "Fractured Love." *These were the songs that were initially going to be the foundation for* Pyromania*'s follow-up.*

Since Mutt Lange was not returning to produce Def Leppard's fourth album, the band attempted to work with Jim Steinman (of Meat Loaf and Bonnie Tyler fame) producing, which is when things began heading downhill.

Joe Elliott described the band's working relationship (or lack thereof) with Steinman back in 1987:

> *"We were a million miles apart in our ideas about sounds, style, timing. And he couldn't adapt to the band. It was a mismatch from the start."*

Joe further elaborated on the band's discontent, and the epiphany they had about Steinman to Billboard.com:

> *"He wrote [Meat Loaf's] 'Bat Out of Hell.' Todd Rundgren produced it, and we quickly learned there was a difference."*

The band went back to the drawing board and tried again, this time attempting to produce the album themselves with the help of Mutt Lange's engineer Nigel Green. But things quickly took an ominous turn when Rick Allen's car accident occurred only weeks into the collaboration.

Everything came to a grinding halt on the project, again.

The irony about Rick's horrific accident is that it afforded Mutt Lange the time to reconsider and return to produce the album.

Mutt's arrival resulted in all the songs initially recorded for the album being scrapped or put on the backburner, so to speak, some subsequently becoming B-sides for what would be *Hysteria*'s future singles. (For instance, "I Wanna Be Your Hero" ended up as the B-side for "Animal.")

The culmination of these events, and all the stops and starts, finally put Def Leppard's fourth album on track to become what would be *Hysteria* and not something more in line with the songs of *Retro Active*.

Mutt Lange: Def Leppard's 6th Member (And More)

Mutt Lange is synonymous with massive, multi-layered productions, and his immersive, indispensable involvement in producing Def Leppard's *Hysteria* is no exception.

Simply put, *Hysteria* (and *Pyromania*) would not be the monumental album it turned out to be without him. Only after Mutt Lange agreed to join the project did it finally begin to take shape.

Mutt's contributions were immense, starting with co-writing every song on *Hysteria*.

The album's exceptional production, which even included an instance of recording one guitar note at a time to capture the perfect sound, was all masterminded by Mutt Lange.

"Love Bites," the first and only #1 single in Def Leppard's career was a Mutt Lange creation. The song's unforgettable backing vocals also prominently feature Mutt's voice.

Guitarist Phil Collen described how "Love Bites" came about in an interview with SongFacts.com:

"[Love Bites] was really a Mutt Lange song - he brought it to us and he played it on an acoustic guitar to me and Steve. It sounded more like the Eagles. He sounds like Don Henley. Mutt's got an amazing voice and most of the backing vocals on that song are actually Mutt singing. We are on there but you can't really hear us -- that's all Mutt's vocals."

Phil also explained the origins of the song "Hysteria," a track which he and bassist Rick Savage initially *thought* had a chorus...until Mutt intervened:

"It started off, we were in Dublin and Rick Savage started playing this tune, so I immediately started singing, 'Out of touch, out of reach.' That was literally the first thing that came out of my mouth. He said that was cool and he goes, [singing] 'I got to know tonight,' this whole other section. We glued it together and we got very excited... We sat down and were playing acoustic guitar, singing over the demo, and we thought that was going to be the chorus. And Mutt Lange said, 'Okay, that's a great verse, a great bridge. Now we need the chorus.' Uh, okay. [Laughs]"

Can you imagine the song "Hysteria" without its classic chorus? On a related note, revisit the song's infectious *"Oh can you feel it? Do you believe* it?" portion: those harmonies are primarily Mutt Lange's signature backing vocals.

In recent years, Phil has spoken more about Mutt's substantial contributions to *Hysteria* and his positive influence on Def Leppard:

"That whole album, [Mutt] really taught us how to sing

and play. I think we'd been an okay band, we'd been a good band, but he made it something great. He deserves all the credit."

Rick Allen's tragic accident was not only devastating, but it could easily have been career-ending, not to mention life-threatening. Mutt Lange helped motivate and inspire Rick to conceive of a completely new approach to drumming via an electronic drum kit, one which incorporated the use of his left leg to compensate for the loss of his left arm.

Rick Allen discussed how the innovative idea came to be in an interview with Billboard.com:

"There were times at the beginning when I really felt like I couldn't do this anymore. The thing that really helped is Mutt came to visit and he talked me into being able to do this but in a different way. I started to figure out on my own the worst thing for me to do was to compare myself to others or compare myself to how I used to play. As soon as I embraced the idea of uniqueness, then I really started to come out of my shell."

These are just *some* of Mutt Lange's immeasurable contributions to *Hysteria* and the band's success.

One more important example: After finally finishing up the recording of *Hysteria*, it was Mutt Lange who approached Joe Elliott upon hearing a catchy melody Joe was messing around with on an acoustic guitar during a studio break.

Joe initially dismissed it, but Mutt insisted they pursue it further, believing a hit song resided within Joe's impromptu jam session. Thus, "Pour Some Sugar On Me" was born, a song that ended up being a game-changer for *Hysteria* and career-changing for the band, taking Def Leppard's popularity to extraordinary heights.

Rick Allen: Tragedy To Triumph

Drummer Rick Allen's unfathomable tragedy of losing an arm not only changed his life but Def Leppard's as well.

The band's sound fundamentally (and inevitably) transformed upon Rick's return, changing and establishing what is now Def Leppard's trademark sound.

Rick's triumphant return to the band not only exemplified how he coped and overcame tragedy, but it also inspired so many others who themselves had lost limbs, suffered hardships, and had to overcome a disability (many of whom Rick would meet with personally, and privately, before shows).

In hindsight, Rick's accident was another example of how the band overcame an incomprehensible challenge and consequently turned it into a positive. On a personal level for Rick, it provided him with a whole new outlook on life.

Rick discussing what his mindset was before the accident is quite revealing:

> "The irony...is that before the accident, I'd pretty much lost interest in playing drums. 'Cause I felt I didn't have anything else to prove as a musician...and boy was I wrong about that one."

Continuing, he discussed how his tragedy actually turned into a blessing *after* the accident:

> "Before my accident, I was a little too...selfish and self-absorbed and for me, to [now] be at the place where I can kind of give back and inspire people. I'm blessed. I'm really blessed."

When Bad Luck Becomes Good Timing

Some of *Hysteria*'s challenges and delays ended up working in the album's *favor*.

Even though "Women" struck out as the album's first single, it laid the groundwork for extending *Hysteria*'s single release strategy. After third single "Hysteria" had peaked, the band's record company had to make a difficult decision: cut their losses on the album and stop promoting it (i.e., don't release any more songs), or spend additional money to release at least one more single to see if it could make a difference.

As legend has it, they chose to release a fourth single: "Pour Some Sugar On Me," which resulted in *Hysteria*'s album sales to skyrocket.

Timing-wise, it worked out perfectly: "Pour Some Sugar On Me" became *the* song of the summer of 1988. Not only that, it breathed new life into *Hysteria* and became the springboard for additional singles -- "Love Bites," "Armageddon It," and "Rocket," which, collectively, sustained the album's momentum into 1989, two and a half years after *Hysteria*'s release!

Other seemingly minor occurrences also contributed to *Hysteria*'s uniqueness, all the result of convenient timing.

"Gods of War" was taken to a whole other sonic level when snippets from speeches by Ronald Reagan and Margaret Thatcher were interspersed throughout the song's climax featuring wartime sound effects. Thanks to a stroke of well-timed political luck, the band (and Mutt Lange) had these speeches at the ready during *Hysteria*'s recording sessions, and it's a good thing they did -- after all, the song's epic finale just wouldn't have been as chill-inducing without the inclusion of quotes like *"They counted on America to be passive. They counted wrong."*

There was another significant event whose timing benefitted *Hysteria* tremendously...

Are You Gettin' It...On CD As Well?

We'll never know how Def Leppard's fourth studio album would have performed had it been released years before its eventual August 1987 date, nor do we know how well it would have sold.

One thing is for sure, though. The introduction of an up-and-coming music format -- the compact disc -- worked to the album's advantage, helping to sustain and further increase *Hysteria*'s sales momentum.

In 1985, compact disc sales were barely a blip, but by 1988, there was a whole new revolution in the music industry when it came to consuming content -- CD sales were approximately 150 million units and growing exponentially!

By 1989, CD sales exceeded 200 million units, approaching 300 million by 1990.

The format created a new sales resurgence for *Hysteria*.

On a related note, there are surely numerous Def Leppard fans who originally purchased *Hysteria* on cassette (maybe twice if they wore out the first one), and then bought yet another copy on CD.

(Early CD packaging)

If there was ever an album worth owning during the technology's infancy, to truly experience its groundbreaking audio capabilities, it would be *Hysteria*; it was a must-have for many CD consumers.

Additionally, the format's ability to squeeze over an hour's worth of music onto a disc did not go unnoticed either, most notably by Mutt Lange.

Phil Collen spoke to *Goldmine* about it:

> *"One of the big things that a lot of people don't realize Mutt was doing with 'Hysteria' was that he was making the album for CD buyers. He knew the CD thing was going to take off..."*

Ultimately, the new format allowed Def Leppard fans to have at least two (love) bites at the *Hysteria* apple.

Final Thoughts

There are many reasons why Def Leppard's *Hysteria* was, is, and always will be such a special release (in addition to the somber reminder that it is Steve Clark's final album with the band).

It took almost a year for it to reach #1 on *Billboard*'s album chart. Remarkably, not only did it claim the top spot for a total of six weeks during its run, but *Hysteria* remained on the chart for 136 weeks.

The album ended up selling 12 million copies in the U.S. alone and over 25 million copies worldwide. An outstanding accomplishment, especially when reminded that the band's average age at the time of its release was approximately 27 years old. (Joe Elliott was 28; Steve Clark, 27; Rick Savage, 26; Phil Collen, 29; Rick Allen, 23.)

Hysteria's early struggles encapsulate many of the things that are still representative of Def Leppard: navigating through challenges, overcoming tragedy, persevering, and triumphantly succeeding. Decades after the album's release, the band continues pressing forward, still making music and selling out venues when touring.

Ever the optimist, here's what Joe Elliott told the *Los Angeles Times* back in 1987, soon after *Hysteria*'s release:

> "All those delays helped the new album. It would have been more in the vein of 'Pyromania,' more than we wanted it to be. With the added time, we've been able to expand our musical horizons. 'Hysteria' has more variety to it and it's more mature."

In the end, the struggles, delays, and hardships the band faced while making their fourth album were not roadblocks.

They were merely a part of what ultimately made *Hysteria* the acclaimed album we continue to celebrate.

Steve Clark: A Tribute

Steve Clark (1960-1991) left such an indelible mark on Def Leppard's legacy.

It's astounding that Steve performed on *only four* of Def Leppard's albums (*On Through The Night*, *High 'n' Dry*, *Pyromania*, and *Hysteria*), which is a testament to the impact he had in shaping the band's music, trademark sound, and, ultimately, its identity.

Even decades after his passing, it's practically impossible to discuss some of Def Leppard's greatest songs without mentioning how Steve Clark played a key role, literally and figuratively: the unmistakable opening riffs of "Photograph" and "Wasted," the guitar introductions to "Gods Of War" and "Foolin'," the unforgettable "Switch 625," and so many other Def Leppard songs Steve co-wrote and performed on.

Without Steve Clark, Def Leppard would not be where it is today, nor would the band have reached the stratospheric heights of success they achieved with *Pyromania* and *Hysteria*.

> "Steve had more swagger than anyone I'd ever seen. His whole thing was that he wasn't a standard player. He'd come up with ideas that other guys wouldn't do. Like the solo in [the song 'Hysteria']... He came up with the whole melody and it almost reminded you of a Japanese garden. It had these weird note choices, really beautiful." --

Phil Collen, MusicRadar.com

Steve was such an integral part of Def Leppard, helping to lay the foundation which the band still stands upon today.

Feelin' Like It's Over...

Def Leppard fundamentally changed on January 8, 1991, the day Steve Clark died.

Fans' hearts sank that day as well when MTV interrupted their regularly scheduled programming with "breaking news" and a graphic of Steve's face on screen. It was confusing, shocking, sad, and so tragic to then hear MTV's Kurt Loder announce the grim news of Steve's death.

In an instant so much changed for the band and its fans.

Aside from the human tragedy of Steve's life ending at the far-too-young age of 30, numerous other, albeit less important, realizations began to sink in over time: Def Leppard lost one of its original, core members; there would be no more 'Terror Twins'; hearing "Photograph" performed live, especially its iconic, opening riff (which was Steve's creation), would *never* be the same; Joe Elliott could no longer playfully call out to Steve with his classic line *"C'mon, Steve. Get it!"* during "Armageddon It," and so on.

Moreover, it was simply hard to fathom Def Leppard without Steve Clark's legendary and irreplaceable on-stage presence.

Bringin' On The Heartbreak

Steve Clark's death occurred in a pre-social media era. As a result, fans didn't have a universal online platform to grieve or even discuss the situation with millions of other heartbroken

Def Leppard fans.

Instead, most were glued to their television sets, watching MTV to get the latest updates, and hoping to hear from the band to share in their loss. (I still recall the image of a very somber Joe Elliott discussing Steve's passing during a follow-up MTV interview.)

Up to that point, Def Leppard fans had been waiting years for the band's follow-up to *Hysteria*, but it all seemed so inconsequential the day Steve died.

All of a sudden, it became a question of *if* or *how* Def Leppard -- a two-guitarist band -- would resume, not what their next album might sound like.

Fortunately, Def Leppard would ultimately persevere, overcoming yet another tragedy.

Stand Up! Kick Steve Into Motion!

Adrenalize was the first Def Leppard album to not feature Steve Clark's guitar contributions on record. (Phil Collen performed all the guitar parts, including Steve's, working off of his original demos as a guide.)

It would have been nice, though, and even a bit therapeutic for heartbroken fans back in the day, to hear *some* of Steve's actual guitar contributions on the record. For instance, an *Adrenalize* gem like "Stand Up! (Kick Love Into Motion)." What was Steve's initial approach to the track? What melodies would he have showcased, and how would he have performed them?

In case you weren't aware, answers to those questions may actually exist, courtesy of a supposed demo of Steve's original guitar solo for "Stand Up! (Kick Love Into Motion)" that has been on the internet for years. Phil Collen reportedly confirmed its existence years ago, saying that the demo is legitimate and that it's him and Steve performing together. Just like the old days.

If you've never heard it before, what may be the emotive melodies of Steve's chill-inducing "Stand Up! (Kick Love Into Motion)" solo can be found on YouTube.

Steve Clark's Legacy

Def Leppard's induction into the Rock & Roll Hall of Fame provided the band with yet another opportunity to look back and reflect on what Steve meant to them, as a band member and friend.

Joe Elliott summed it up beautifully in his very poignant acceptance speech:

> "It was Pete [Willis], after a chance meeting in a college canteen, both reaching for the same guitar magazine, who introduced us to the late, great Steve Clark. Over the following 10 years, Steve made a massive musical contribution to this band, his incredible and unique riffs helped shape some of the most important songs we will ever write and it really does go without saying that we love him and we miss him every day."

The band has mentioned in interviews over the years that unreleased material from Steve *does* exist. One can only hope they release it someday.

Hearing material like the "Stand Up! (Kick Love Into Motion)" guitar demo is a nice reminder that though Steve may be gone, his presence remains. And though he will never be part of any new music Def Leppard records, Steve is undoubtedly still with the band in spirit, playing along with his Gibson Les Paul guitar slung low, riffing as only he can.

Much has been said about Steve in many fine, well-deserved tributes over the years, whether spotlighting his personal ups and downs, the demons he fought, and so on. But what I prefer to think about when I'm reminded of Stephen Maynard Clark, no matter the anniversary, is simply the exceptional work he left behind.

Def Leppard and its fans were so fortunate to witness Steve's genius in the short amount of time he was with us. Though forever missed, Steve and his immeasurable contributions will never be forgotten.

Thank you, Steve.

Album Spotlight: *Adrenalize*

Def Leppard's fifth studio album *Adrenalize* was released in March 1992.

It had been 5 very long years since previous album *Hysteria* was released, which brought the band immense commercial success, a world tour that lasted years, and when all was said and done, a lingering question: What's next?

What kind of release would the band come up with to follow up *Hysteria*, an album that handily outsold its blockbuster predecessor, *Pyromania*, and was now one of the biggest selling rock albums in history?

Add to the equation that Def Leppard's pseudo-sixth member Mutt Lange was *not* going to be the new album's producer, and the pressure -- mostly self-imposed by the band -- to develop *Hysteria*'s successor was all but certain to mount.

Incidentally, Mutt Lange's parting advice to the band was to *not* attempt to create an album in the vein of *Hysteria*, and to go in a completely different direction.

Rick Savage explained the situation to *Classic Rock* magazine:

> "It was obvious Mutt wasn't going to be a hands-on producer, like he'd been on the previous three albums. He said, 'You know what you should do – you should forget about doing a 'Hysteria'-type album and make a Guns

N' Roses-type album.' We didn't know how to take that."

No Promises, No Guarantees

Any questions regarding the creative direction of Def Leppard's fifth studio album came to a halt and quickly became unimportant when the band had to cope with yet another tragedy: the death of Steve Clark.

Eventually, a whole new set of questions would arise and need to be addressed, this time about the band itself: Is there a path forward without Steve Clark, whose contributions to Def Leppard were incalculable? Would the band proceed as a four-piece? Can the band survive this latest tragedy?

From Tragedy To Triumph, Again

Ultimately, Def Leppard overcame the momentous setback of Steve Clark's death, persevering and thriving, as their latest album, *Adrenalize,* became yet another #1 release, selling millions of copies around the world.

Many fans longing for the band's return, especially after such a long hiatus, welcomed Def Leppard back with open arms. Radio stations, on the other hand, needed more convincing, as the music industry and radio listeners' preferences were increasingly veering towards grunge music in the '90s.

As a result, extra efforts were made early on to "reintroduce" Def Leppard and answer some inevitable questions.

A special, promotional interview CD was created by the band's record company and mailed out to radio stations, to not only help promote the *Adrenalize* release but also address questions surrounding the status of the band.

The interview disc featured a booklet that included a list of questions; the CD's tracks simply included Joe Elliott's recorded answers to those questions.

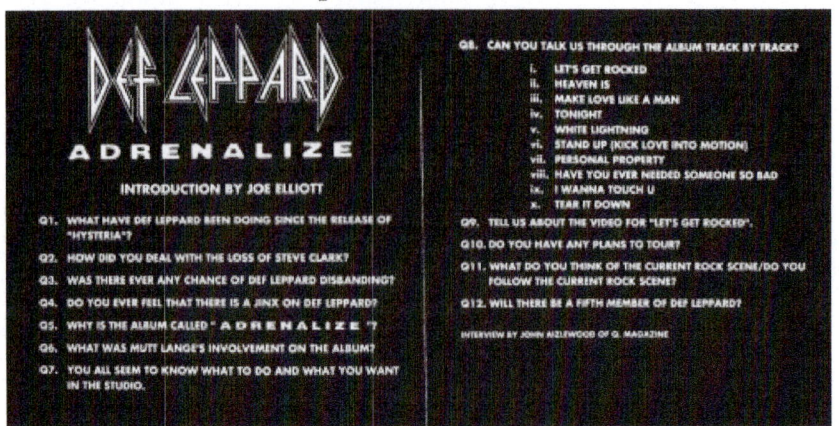

```
DEF LEPPARD
ADRENALIZE
INTRODUCTION BY JOE ELLIOTT

Q1. WHAT HAVE DEF LEPPARD BEEN DOING SINCE THE RELEASE OF "HYSTERIA"?
Q2. HOW DID YOU DEAL WITH THE LOSS OF STEVE CLARK?
Q3. WAS THERE EVER ANY CHANCE OF DEF LEPPARD DISBANDING?
Q4. DO YOU EVER FEEL THAT THERE IS A JINX ON DEF LEPPARD?
Q5. WHY IS THE ALBUM CALLED "ADRENALIZE"?
Q6. WHAT WAS MUTT LANGE'S INVOLVEMENT ON THE ALBUM?
Q7. YOU ALL SEEM TO KNOW WHAT TO DO AND WHAT YOU WANT IN THE STUDIO.

Q8. CAN YOU TALK US THROUGH THE ALBUM TRACK BY TRACK?
  i. LET'S GET ROCKED
  ii. HEAVEN IS
  iii. MAKE LOVE LIKE A MAN
  iv. TONIGHT
  v. WHITE LIGHTNING
  vi. STAND UP (KICK LOVE INTO MOTION)
  vii. PERSONAL PROPERTY
  viii. HAVE YOU EVER NEEDED SOMEONE SO BAD
  ix. I WANNA TOUCH U
  x. TEAR IT DOWN
Q9. TELL US ABOUT THE VIDEO FOR "LET'S GET ROCKED".
Q10. DO YOU HAVE ANY PLANS TO TOUR?
Q11. WHAT DO YOU THINK OF THE CURRENT ROCK SCENE/DO YOU FOLLOW THE CURRENT ROCK SCENE?
Q12. WILL THERE BE A FIFTH MEMBER OF DEF LEPPARD?

INTERVIEW BY JOHN AIZLEWOOD OF Q. MAGAZINE
```

Even knowing how things turned out, it's still captivating to hear some of Joe's responses in hindsight. For example, question #12: "Will there be a fifth member of Def Leppard?"

Here's an excerpt from Joe's answer:

> *"Yes, there will be a fifth Leppard. We don't know who it is...We just gotta make sure we get the right guy. We've got a few people in mind...The most important thing is they're British and that they're a very nice guy."*

The disc also included a track-by-track breakdown of *Adrenalize*'s songs (who better to promote a new Def Leppard album to radio stations than Joe himself?) which included some interesting tidbits.

For example, Rick Allen originally came up with the idea for "I Wanna Touch U," but the song's opening verse was actually based on a chorus Joe had written for a *completely different* song tentatively titled "High Over You," which was later changed to "High On You." That song title ended up being the first line for "I Wanna Touch U." (*"I get high on you...!"*)

In At The Deep End, Hang On Tight

Adrenalize featured several memorable tracks. "Let's Get Rocked" is still a fan favorite; "Have You Ever Needed Someone So Bad" remains one of the band's biggest power ballads; other gems like "Stand Up (Kick Love Into Motion)" and the album's epic "White Lightning" continue to be ever-popular.

To this day, *Adrenalize* remains the only album Def Leppard recorded as a four-piece (also seen in the band's "Let's Get Rocked" music video).

Arguably, in retrospect, *Adrenalize*'s single release strategy was not as effective as it could have been. For instance, should "Make Love Like A Man" have been the *second* single off the album, and should it have been a single release at all? (See the chapter spotlighting the song for more on that.)

Moreover, "Tonight" was the *third* ballad off the album released as a single. For various reasons, this too was a misstep. (See the "Tonight" song spotlight chapter for more.)

Looking Back

Being such a unique, trying time, it's understandable that the band has mixed feelings about *Adrenalize*, even to this day.

Rick Savage had this somber yet candid reflection about the album (included in Def Leppard's 2015 *Classic Rock Presents* Fanpack):

> "We tried to outdo Hysteria, which was a mistake…It really doesn't cut it for me."

Meanwhile, Joe Elliott has stated that his opinion about the album changes constantly, from not liking it to considering it a "cool, glam rock" album.

Final Thoughts

Inevitably, Def Leppard was a changed band with the *Adrenalize* release. Regardless of your opinion of the album, the band unquestionably overcame yet another tragedy, persevered, and continued on in their quest to tour the world and entertain audiences.

Joe Elliott is famously known for saying at the end of Def Leppard's concerts, "Don't forget us, we won't forget you!" The phrase seems all the more appropriate when reflecting on the band's challenging *Adrenalize* era.

Fortunately, Def Leppard was not forgotten by fans, and it felt good to have the band back.

Album Spotlight: *Retro Active*

Def Leppard's *Retro Active* album was released in October 1993.

What's Old Is New

The year was 1993. Def Leppard had released their fifth original studio album *Adrenalize* the year before, which performed extremely well early on but notably began losing sales momentum in the months that followed. The album would go on to sell four million copies in the U.S. alone -- an impressive achievement but nowhere near the sales heights of previous releases *Hysteria* and *Pyromania*.

Arnold Schwarzenegger's latest movie *Last Action Hero* was being released that summer. Def Leppard had been approached about contributing a song to the film's soundtrack, but due to the band's ceaseless touring in support of *Adrenalize* -- a tour that would last nearly a year and a half -- they didn't have the time to record a new song. So they ended up sending over a leftover B-side from their *Adrenalize* recording sessions for consideration, a Joe Elliott-penned ballad titled "Two Steps Behind."

Not only would the track end up on the *Last Action Hero* soundtrack, but a new layer of orchestral strings (courtesy of music conductor Michael Kamen) was added on to further sweeten and enhance Def Leppard's song offering.

Being a part of an Arnold Schwarzenegger summer film presented a great opportunity, at least until critics' reviews and word-of-mouth panned it, resulting in the movie grossly underperforming box office expectations in the U.S.

As for the placement of "Two Steps Behind" in the film, moviegoers and Def Leppard fans would have to wait...and wait...to hear it, as it was slotted at the very end -- not even in the movie portion, but deep into the end credits.

From a marketing and publicity perspective, it was a great selling point to tout that Def Leppard's song would be included in Arnold's latest movie, but having it appear so late in the film -- literally, when most of the audience had already left the theater -- was disappointing.

Nevertheless, there was a bright spot: The soundtrack, featuring acts such as AC/DC, Megadeth, Tesla, Aerosmith, and Def Leppard was a hit, unlike the film, and ended up going platinum, helping bring added awareness to "Two Steps Behind."

The song ended up peaking at an impressive #12 on *Billboard*'s Hot 100 singles chart. For comparison, "Have You Ever Needed Someone So Bad" also peaked at #12 on the same chart a year earlier; only "Love Bites" charted higher in terms of Def Leppard ballads. (Though not realized at the time, "Two Steps Behind" would be the band's last major hit single, in terms of mainstream, Top 20 chart performance.)

The impact of "Two Steps Behind" went beyond its chart achievement, though, as it resulted in something even more significant: its success inspired Def Leppard to put together a compilation album filled with B-sides and other previously unreleased material.

This brings us to *Retro Active*.

Def Leppard's *Retro Active*

Retro Active featured an eclectic mix of material, including B-sides, newly recorded tracks, and even alternate versions of songs. The unique compilation was also noteworthy for another reason: it provided the opportunity for the band to reflect *and* close the book on a previous era, most notably the Steve Clark years.

Retro Active's release occurred about a year after guitarist Vivian Campbell joined Def Leppard, so what better time to release a collection of material that included remnants of Steve's work to add a bit of closure.

In the end, there wasn't a lot of "unreleased" material on *Retro Active* that was entirely new or never heard before, at least to Def Leppard music collectors. That being said, "Desert Song" and "Fractured Love" were two newly introduced gems.

As for most of the other tracks on the compilation, previous versions had already been released, whether as B-sides on singles from the *Hysteria* album, or songs that were included on international releases of *Adrenalize*.

Retro Active Track Breakdown

Putting aside minor remixes and overdubbing tweaks that were done for the album, here's a quick recap of where *Retro Active*'s songs had already been available prior to its release:

- **Desert Song**

    New track (from the *Hysteria* era), never released until *Retro Active*.

- **Fractured Love**

    New track (from the *Hysteria* era), never released until *Retro Active*.

- **Action**

    A cover of a Sweet song, previously released as a B-side on the "Make Love Like A Man" single.

- **Two Steps Behind (Acoustic)**

Released first on the *Last Action Hero* soundtrack (with orchestral strings added), also a B-side on the "Make Love Like A Man" single.

- **She's Too Tough**

Previously released as a bonus track on the Japanese release of *Adrenalize*, also a B-side on the "Tonight" single.

- **Miss You In A Heartbeat**

Previously released as a bonus track on the Japanese version of *Adrenalize*, also released as a B-side on the "Make Love Like A Man" single. (A previous version of the song was also released years earlier by a band named The Law.)

- **Only After Dark**

A cover of a Mick Ronson song, previously released as a B-side on the "Let's Get Rocked" single.

- **Ride Into The Sun**

Previously released as a B-side on the "Hysteria" single.

- **From The Inside**

Previously released as a B-side on the "Have You Ever Needed Someone So Bad" single.

- **Ring of Fire**

Previously released as a B-side on the "Pour Some Sugar On Me" single.

- **I Wanna Be Your Hero**

Previously released as a B-side on the "Animal" single.

- **Miss You In A Heartbeat (Electric version)**

"Electric version" new for *Retro Active*.

- **Two Steps Behind (Electric version)**

"Electric version" new for *Retro Active*.

- **Miss You In A Heartbeat (Piano version)**

"Piano version" new (hidden) track for *Retro Active*.

While the vast majority of songs were previously available in some form or another, *Retro Active* was still a solid compilation, especially for Def Leppard fans who never collected the band's earlier releases and missed out on that material.

Release Strategy

Even as a one-off compilation, *Retro Active* included tracks that were radio-friendly and worthy of single consideration. Unfortunately, the album's single release strategy was not optimal and didn't maximize its commercial appeal.

After several *Adrenalize* single missteps the previous year, which in part contributed to the album's sales to stall and never quite recover, there was hope *Retro Active* could right some of those wrongs.

"Two Steps Behind" was already a well-known track courtesy of the *Last Action Hero* soundtrack, which was released about *four months* before *Retro Active*. Even though the song was officially released as a single in August 1993, if fans wanted to own it immediately -- and many certainly did -- they could have purchased a cassingle, CD single, or bought the readily available *Last Action Hero* soundtrack.

Buying *Retro Active* simply wasn't an option, since it still hadn't been released.

So right off the bat, the wind was taken out of *Retro Active*'s commercial sails -- and, more specifically, sales -- since what was likely the most mainstream track on the album was available for purchase elsewhere. (Of course, that doesn't mean hardcore Def Leppard fans still weren't looking forward to *Retro Active*'s forthcoming release; even those who already had most of the compilation's tracks in their collection were still eagerly awaiting new tracks "Fractured Love" and "Desert Song.")

Radio Strategy

While "Desert Song" was tailor-made for album-oriented rock radio (AOR) stations, "Fractured Love" was the more radio-ready track of the two, packing a powerful punch with a hard rock sound that immediately harkened back to the band's *Pyromania* era.

"Desert Song" was promoted to AOR radio stations the month of *Retro Active*'s release, and it reached a respectable #12 position on *Billboard*'s niche Mainstream Rock Tracks chart.

As for standout track "Fractured Love," it was never released as a single or focus track, not even to rock stations. ("Action" was not released in the U.S. either, but was a single in the U.K., peaking at #14.)

Retro Active's U.S. promotional strategy was ultimately comprised of "Two Steps Behind" (a single which benefited the *Last Action Hero* soundtrack most), a limited push to AOR stations for "Desert Song," and one additional single: the ballad "Miss You In A Heartbeat," which would peak at #39 on *Billboard*'s Hot 100 singles chart, the last time a Def Leppard single would crack that chart's Top 40.

Again, *Retro Active* signified the end of a Def Leppard era, one the band would never return to due to Steve Clark's death, and featured several tracks from the "Steve years." "Fractured Love" (co-written by Steve Clark) would have emphatically put an exclamation point on the closing of that Def Leppard chapter.

Regrettably, the rock aspect of *Retro Active* was mostly

brushed aside, as the two official singles chosen to promote the album were ballads ("Two Steps Behind" and "Miss You In A Heartbeat").

And while *Retro Active* was not a new original studio album, and the band was still touring in support of *Adrenalize* -- which had been out about a year and a half by this point, with all of its singles released -- it could have effectively provided Def Leppard with a more substantial tailwind.

"Two Steps Behind" Music Video

Retro Active's most well-known music video, "Two Steps Behind," centered around Joe Elliott walking down a street while everyone and everything around him appeared to move backward. It was a neat, memorable visual. (In reality, Joe was filmed walking backward while the action around him occurred normally.)

The video was then topped off with live footage of the band performing the song in front of a concert audience. (The ballad lives on to this day, most notably in acoustic form, as Def Leppard frequently performs it on tour.)

The song's alternate "electric version" was more of a one-off to offer a little more variety and freshness to *Retro Active*; the only time it received any type of promotional push was during a short TV spot in 1993, which the band filmed for *Monday Night Football*.

Undoubtedly, it was fun for fans to see the guys playing ball (and refer to a football as a "saw-seege"), but the spot was far too short to make a lasting, meaningful impression on viewers.

"Miss You In A Heartbeat" Music Video

One of the most memorable aspects of the "Miss You In A

Heartbeat" music video was offering fans a peek into some of the band member's homes. For example, Joe Elliott played piano and sang in his living room, while Rick Savage played bass from the comfort of his own home, as Rick Allen supplied the drumming from his residence.

It was a unique approach, but also exposed the fact that the band wasn't performing the song together. Having everyone's portions filmed separately resulted in having to rely on post-production editing and technical tricks to provide more fluidity to the band's performance.

Hence, Joe performing alone in his living room resulted in Sav's footage appearing in Joe's window and footage of Phil Collen appearing on the living room floor, beneath Joe's feet. Meanwhile, Vivian Campbell's footage appeared in Sav's window, as Rick Allen's portion was beamed onto a wall.

Making the footage of each band members' performance work together succeeded for the most part, but, frankly, also came across as lackluster and low budget at times, especially when the video would periodically superimpose Joe Elliott's translucent face over outdoor scenery to help maintain some semblance of continuity.

It was quite apparent the video was filmed while the band was on break, with each member enjoying time off on their own. Thus, a quick video shoot of them dutifully performing their respective parts for the video would have to suffice.

It's certainly not a poor result, but it could have been executed better. Much better. (But, hey, check out those beautiful, scenic views!)

The Album Cover

Retro Active's album cover was inspired by artist Charles Allan Gilbert and his 1892 piece "All is Vanity," which featured a woman seated at a vanity table, looking at herself in the mirror.

When viewed from a distance, the woman and her surroundings create the eerie illusion of a human skull.

The visual is effective and memorable, and especially apropos for *Retro Active* and its purpose.

Final Thoughts

Retro Active debuted at #9 on *Billboard*'s album chart and went on to reach platinum status. Not including Def Leppard's greatest hits releases *Vault* and *Rock of Ages: The Definitive Collection*, *Retro Active* would be the band's last "new" studio release to achieve platinum sales certification.

Ultimately, *Retro Active* accomplished what the band set out to do: Put out an album of mostly older material to close the book on an era they wanted -- and needed -- to move on from. Soon afterward, the band would venture into new, uncharted territory to create what would be their *Slang* album.

Even though *Retro Active* put an end to Def Leppard's Steve Clark chapter, it's virtually impossible to leave behind Steve's legacy and incalculable contributions. A fitting lyric from "Two Steps Behind" comes to mind: *"You can run but you can never hide, from the shadow that's creepin' up beside you."* Likewise, Steve Clark's impact will always be a fundamental part of Def Leppard.

And while *Retro Active* was a compilation primarily celebrating Steve Clark and the band's earlier work, it's still a solid standalone release that echoes an earlier Def Leppard era while still sounding contemporary, even to this day.

Peeks Inside *Vault's* Vault & More!

I still have "advanced" pre-release copies of Def Leppard albums on audio cassette, which would typically be distributed around the band's record label's offices. These versions arrived so far in advance of the album's official release that the cassette sleeve wouldn't even include the cover artwork, just text that included the album's tracklisting. (CD copies hadn't been pressed yet.)

For example, here's the one for *Vault*:

It was always a thrill to pop an advanced cassette into the

office stereo system's cassette deck (or my car radio's cassette player at the time) and hear what truly was brand-spankin' new music, while also having no idea whatsoever about what you were about to hear -- there weren't any PR or marketing campaigns in effect yet to position the release or provide you with details and context about the songs it contained.

Playing these early cassettes for the very first time was a treat no matter who the artist was -- be it Bon Jovi, KISS, The Scorpions, U2 (on a sister record label), etc.

Actually, back then there were times when Def Leppard-related products would arrive in the office mail on a fairly regular basis, which wasn't all that uncommon if a new release was on the horizon.

Like receiving a *Slang* travel bag...

Or a VHS copy of a music video that had just been filmed -- in some cases, it would be so hot off the press that a note would be handwritten on the cassette's label making it clear that what you're receiving is a "Rough Cut!" and not the final version...

Sometimes a promotional item would arrive hyping the title of a new single on it, whether it be a t-shirt or even a small towel...

After receiving an album's advanced cassette, CD copies stamped "For Promotional Use Only" would follow in due time, with the allotment likely revealing the album cover's final artwork.

Here's a promo-stamped CD example (which the band signed for me)...

Not long after that, more promo CDs would show up, except this time around they would only contain a particular track or single for radio stations to focus on for airplay consideration.

Here's a sampling of these types of promotional CDs...

The thin cardboard CD sleeve was not only supposed to be eye-catching but also convenient to quickly mail out in a small padded envelope to radio stations, accounts (i.e., to buyers who purchase quantities for their stores), press outlets, etc.

Sometimes promotional product was simply a CD in a clear case since accompanying artwork wasn't available. It could be a song sampler for a soon-to-be-released album or an upcoming single or focus track for radio stations. One example is "Desert Song," which was sent out to AOR stations. Another example is "Two Steps Behind," where both versions -- the electric and acoustic -- were included on a disc. (Clearly, the acoustic version was much preferred over the electric by radio stations who supported the track.)

Subsequent incoming office deliveries would include copies of a music video's final version. Sometimes an EPK (electronic press kit) would also arrive (on VHS), which featured band members discussing the release, providing backstories on songs for their latest album, etc.

All of these types of relics are still part of my Def Leppard collection, in addition to other "atypical" memorabilia, which I always found extra appealing.

If it isn't already apparent from reading some of the album and single spotlight chapters in this book, I consider sales and marketing strategies -- i.e., how the album or single was promoted -- just as significant and worthy of analysis as any other aspect surrounding the release. It genuinely interests me; it did then and still does now.

That being said, some items within my collection which I value just as much as other keepsakes simply involve...information.

For example, the official marketing plan for a Def Leppard album which lays the groundwork for the release: what it's all about, what the current music landscape is, what plans are being put in place to best promote it.

I still find it interesting to look back on this type of archaic information, revisiting what the music industry climate was for the band at that particular moment in time, and how much it has changed since then. It's kind of like unearthing a time capsule that was buried a long time ago. E-mail wasn't even utilized during this time; marketing plans like the ones I'm referring to were sent out for "immediate" distribution...by fax.

Here is the 1995 marketing plan for Def Leppard's *Vault* release from my collection:

fax transmittal

date: October 17, 1995

re: DEF MARKETING PLAN

I thought I'd share a few nostalgic tidbits from it which I think you'll find interesting, but before doing so, I must take a slight detour to discuss one *Vault*-related item that irked me back in the day. And it has nothing to do with the album itself.

Here we go...

By 1995, the depth (and success) of Def Leppard's catalog was indisputable. A "greatest hits" release made perfect sense and was a long time coming -- maybe longer than necessary: *Vault* wasn't released until about *one year* after label-mate Bon Jovi received the same greatest hits treatment.

Nothing against Bon Jovi, but *optically* it seemed like there was potentially a lack of confidence in going with Def Leppard first. Regardless if it was inadvertent, it positioned Def Leppard as jumping onto the Bon Jovi greatest hits bandwagon once *Vault*'s time finally came.

Let me expand on this rationale and further explain.

Bon Jovi enjoyed great success with their greatest hits release, which wasn't at all surprising, but at the time, the strategy for the release came across like this (solely my interpretation):

> *Let's put out a greatest hits compilation of Bon Jovi songs just in time for the holiday season! It should also include at least one new track to further upsell it -- a power ballad would be great and a sure-fire single!*

It wouldn't be until about *a year later* that Def Leppard would finally get their own greatest hits release (giving the notion that Bon Jovi's *Cross Road* greatest hits album had safely paved the way).

Not only that, Def Leppard's release strategy would follow the same formula. Again, my interpretation:

> *Let's go the greatest hits route again, this time with Def*

> Leppard: have the compilation come out in time for the holiday season -- just like Bon Jovi's "Cross Road" -- and have it feature a new track that's a ballad -- just like Bon Jovi's "Cross Road" -- which would also make for a potent single opportunity -- just like Bon Jovi's "Cross Road," etc.

Unintentional or not, this gave the impression of being a copycat approach: whereas Bon Jovi released their greatest hits album *Cross Road* in October 1994, Def Leppard released their greatest hits album *Vault* in October 1995; Bon Jovi's featured new track and single was the ballad "Always"; Def Leppard's featured new track and single was the ballad "When Love & Hate Collide." (I'm starting to get flashbacks from the movie *Coming To America*, comparing the Big Mac and the Big Mick!)

Now, I completely understand the "if it ain't broke, don't fix it" approach, but timing-wise -- again, at least *optically* -- it seemed unfair to Def Leppard (or at least to this Def Leppard fan), as it appeared that the band was not only following in someone else's footsteps *to a tee* but also *needed* them to lead the way.

Furthermore, releasing Def Leppard's greatest hits compilation one year *further* into the '90s -- a decade that unquestionably was becoming increasingly unwelcoming to the band's music with each passing year -- seemed unnecessary and arguably had a negative impact: *Cross Road* debuted in the Top 10 on the U.S. album charts; *Vault* debuted in the Top 15. "Always" became a huge U.S. hit, peaking at #3 on *Billboard*'s Hot 100 singles chart. As for "When Love & Hate Collide"? It didn't even reach the Top 50, *peaking* at an unremarkable #58.

Would "When Love & Hate Collide," a leftover from the *Adrenalize* recording sessions, have performed better had it been released a year earlier? Better yet, is there a case to be made that the song performed better because it was released further into the '90s? I digress.

Ultimately, *Vault* did just fine over the long term -- actually, better than fine -- selling millions of copies, matching and even surpassing *Cross Road*'s U.S. album sales.

I still have my locked, early promotional copy of the CD release!

Now back to the original *Vault* marketing plan...

Here are some glimpses you might find amusing, especially decades after its release.

The opening objective was spot-on...

Objectives

Def Leppard will continue to create Pop/Rock music way into the next century and '*Vault*' highlights the first chapter in an ongoing story. The package will serve as a reminder of the incredible career this band has enjoyed so far. Rather than be a collection of old photos and memorable moments, the album has been designed to look extremely modern & contemporary to emphasize the continuing importance of the songs and the band.

The plan made note of *Vault*'s initial sales goal: 500,000 copies (350,000 CDs and 150,000 Cassettes). Done and then some!

Album Solicitation

Initial quota: CD: (8A)=350,000   Cassette:(T)=150,000
Initial sales goal = 500,000
Solicitation Begins: 9/5   Solicitation Ends: 10/6.

Ad sales strategies targeted various types of music stores ("racks, major chains, regional chains...independent stores"). Obviously, this was long before digital music was considered a popular option, and way before record stores became a rarity!

> The bulk of the co-op plan will be focused on November/December and January programs in the racks, major chains, regional chains and the independent stores, where Def Leppard has Soundscanned well.

The plan was to promote the "When Love & Hate Collide" music video on MTV, even while acknowledging that the network was no longer the go-to promotional vehicle it used to be.

VIDEO PROMOTION

> We are discussing a launch strategy with MTV now. Although Def Leppard is no longer a core artist for MTV, they have had continued exposure on the network. "Let's Get Rocked", "Have You Ever Needed Someone So Bad" and "Two Steps Behind" were all top 5 most requested videos on MTV in the 90's. The gameplan is to position the band as one of the several mainstream Pop/Rock artists that help balance out a playlist filled with "Alternative" and "Urban" artists.

Vault's TV advertising campaign initially targeted (i.e., focused on at least for consideration) only a few, select outlets including ESPN/ESPN 2, TNT, and MTV's shows "Unplugged," "Singled Out," and "Beavis & Butthead" (a show that would eventually make fun of Def Leppard and its music). Another option considered was that year's *Billboard* Music Awards. This game plan is further indicative of the promotional challenges faced at the time, and the limited opportunities available to effectively promote a new Def Leppard album in the mid-'90s.

> Here's a look at the targeted programs cable networks and programs;
>
> MTV: Unplugged, Beavis and Butthead, Singled Out.
> ESPN, ESPN 2 & TNT: Football
> Billboard Music Awards

Hope you enjoyed this little trip down *Vault*'s memory lane! As you can see, the times were most definitely a-changing for Def Leppard during this period.

Fortunately, the quality of *Vault* hasn't changed at all. The music remains as good as it was then!

Album Spotlight: *Slang*

Def Leppard's *Slang* album was released in May 1996.

With the possible exception of *On Through The Night*, *Slang* is arguably the band's most polarizing album.

Upon its release, it was difficult for some longtime fans to accept (at least favorably) that *Slang* didn't sound at all like Def Leppard's previous releases. Where were the anthemic, arena-rocking, chorus-chanting, "sugar"-to-the-ears songs? How about a customary power ballad? Was it possible that a Def Leppard album could *not* prominently feature those things?

With *Slang*, it was.

Grunge music was ruling playlists and charts during this time, and for many radio stations and "previous" Def Leppard fans (as odd as that may sound), it all of a sudden became cool to *not* like the band's music, past or present, and even ridicule it.

By the same token, MTV, once a staunch supporter of the band, changed its format and was now airing series like "Beavis and Butt-Head," a show whose main characters would watch Def Leppard's "Animal" video in one particular episode and comment, *"Spinal Tap really sucks lately!"*

Welcome to the mid-'90s!

Do You Wanna Get...Slanged?

Def Leppard was in a no-win situation: if the band was to release an album with songs remotely resembling tracks like "Pour Some Sugar On Me," many would contend they were stuck in the '80s and out of touch; if they were to go in a grunge-like creative direction, they'd be accused of being inauthentic and copycats of the alternative bands who stole their spotlight.

Put simply: Damned if they do, damned if they don't.

But this didn't happen overnight. When *Adrenalize* was released in 1992, many radio stations that *used to* play Def Leppard's music were beginning to switch formats, as the groundswell for grunge became inescapable. (Fortunately, *Adrenalize* was still able to break through due to strong sales out of the box; the album's massive tour helped support the release, too.)

But peoples' music tastes were unquestionably changing during the *Adrenalize* years.

One prime example was Def Leppard's 1992 performance at MTV's Music Video Awards, which began to uncover a chasm between the band's music and MTV's newly "hip" audience. Being on stage performing "Let's Get Rocked" and shouting out lyrics to the audience about "mowing the lawn" and "tidying your room" just wasn't working out so well.

Things just seemed...off.

Joe Elliott appearing in a rather unique, un-Leppard-like outfit, comprised of biker shorts and a dead mouse/skull t-shirt, capped off with a beret and what looked to be a bathrobe, didn't seem to help the situation either, as evidenced by the rather muted, oft-put crowd response.

Slang With Me...Or Not

By the time of *Slang*'s release in 1996, large segments of Def Leppard's "casual" fans from the late '80s -- especially those who came aboard during *Hysteria*'s heyday -- had completely lost interest in the band. They now preferred groups like Nirvana, Soundgarden, and Alice in Chains.

This was the music landscape Def Leppard was up against.

Not only that, it was a challenging time for band members on a personal level, as hardships and life changes inevitably had to be dealt with: Rick Savage had been diagnosed with Bell's palsy between the *Adrenalize* and *Slang* releases; his father had also passed away. Joe Elliott, Rick Allen, and Phil Collen also had their share of marital/personal issues.

It was a trying time, to put it mildly. (Joe Elliott would go on to describe *Slang* as the album that brought "life into the equation.")

All I Ever Wanna Get Is...*Slang*?

Promoting the *Slang* album was a whole other dilemma.

While some radio stations no longer had any interest in playing (i.e., supporting) anything resembling Def Leppard's brand of music, others stations that still played some form of "rock" had alternative-music-leaning audiences who didn't necessarily want to hear Def Leppard.

The situation became even more challenging when the band's record company didn't have unequivocal, radio-friendly hit singles to choose from to launch the album: there was no "Pour Some Sugar On Me" sequel, not even tongue-in-cheek anthems like "Armageddon It," "Let's Get Rocked," or "Make Love Like A Man."

Moreover, *Slang* featured a stripped-down production; it wasn't recorded in a typical recording studio setting but primarily at a house in Marbella, Spain. Other divergences included Rick Allen using an acoustic drum kit for the project, and Mutt Lange having no production or songwriting involvement.

The *Slang* album cover didn't even showcase Def Leppard's iconic logo or burst with vibrant colors, nor did it involve the band's usual go-to graphic designer, Andie Airfix.

But this was all done intentionally. The band knew *Slang* was a complete departure from previous Def Leppard albums, *especially* the most commercially successful ones, so much so that the band joked that *Slang*'s original working album title was "Commercial Suicide."

Here's how Joe Elliott described the band's thought process for *Slang*:

> "We couldn't just go out there and make an album sounding like Nirvana. That'd be ridiculous. That would have been like cashing in, bandwagon-style. But what we did do is just strip back a lot of the harmony stuff and just made a much more lyrically honest record."

Slang Promotional Strategy

The majority of *Slang*'s songs were written by one or two band members (a creative approach Def Leppard would repeat on future release *Songs from the Sparkle Lounge*).

"Work It Out" was chosen as *Slang*'s all-important first U.S. single, designated to do the heavy lifting of launching the album -- a surprising choice, as the song arguably would have been considered more of a deep cut in prior years.

Solely written by Vivian Campbell, the song's original version was "Leppard-ized" to an extent, yet still featured a distinctly different sound and vibe than what Def Leppard fans were accustomed to. (As mentioned in this book's *Slang* album song ranking, the promotional strategy for "Work It Out" was unconventional; the song was played for some radio station program directors *without* telling them who the band was, just letting the music -- featuring Joe Elliott's relatively unrecognizable Iggy Pop-like vocals -- speak for itself.)

Ultimately, *some* radio stations were pleasantly surprised at the fact that it was a Def Leppard song and did end up supporting the "Work It Out" single, but it didn't result in the heavy airplay rotation the band routinely enjoyed in years past.

The band's music videos for *Slang* prominently had a more somber tone too: "Work It Out" had a serious look and feel, while "All I Want Is Everything" was in the vein of the band's dark, moody "Tonight" music video, with shots of the band intercut throughout its solemn storyline.

Only "Slang" had a music video that was playful, not to mention visually kinetic, but it was mostly enjoyed by international audiences, as it was rarely seen in the U.S.

Slang's Reception

The typical press outlets that normally would have been relied upon to heavily promote a new Def Leppard album just weren't as willing anymore.

And with MTV no longer being a viable, promotional outlet, *Slang* got a fraction of the television coverage the band would have ordinarily received for an album release.

Def Leppard did appear on "The Tonight Show with Jay Leno" to perform "Work It Out" -- surprisingly, the band's first appearance on the late-night program -- but major promotional opportunities were still far and few.

That's not to say there wasn't a lot of interest and coverage elsewhere around the world. There were some terrific interviews with the band that promoted *Slang* effectively, just not in the U.S.

There was an in-depth program that featured the band discussing the *Slang* album, including answering fan questions and taking part in *numerous* interviews. For example, interview segments included Joe and Sav, Joe and Phil, Joe and Rick, Joe and Vivian, and then the entire band together, capped off with showing *Slang* tour rehearsal footage. This excellent promotional vehicle actually aired on MTV...in Europe.

Slang Sales

It's not all that shocking that *Slang* was not a #1 album for Def Leppard, like its predecessors *Hysteria* and *Adrenalize*.

The release debuted at #14 on *Billboard*'s U.S. album chart, selling 59,500 copies in its first week, a far cry from the 380,000 copies previous album *Adrenalize* sold in its debut week. (To put things further into perspective, *Adrenalize* sold over 100,000 copies in *each of its first six weeks* of release.)

But the fact that Def Leppard was still able to achieve a Top 15 album debut in the mid-'90s, with decidedly less radio and press willing to support it, is an accomplishment.

Slang ultimately ended up being certified gold, selling over 500,000 copies.

Def Leppard also released a *Slang* deluxe edition in 2014 and loaded it up with bonus tracks -- demos, alternate versions, and more. The reissue provided the band with a great opportunity to once again spotlight and reflect on a release that just never seemed to find its audience or get its due.

Final Thoughts

It's regrettable that many "casual" Def Leppard fans fled around the time of *Slang*, or simply didn't give the album a fair chance. They missed out on some excellent music that not only showcased *Slang*'s depth but some of the band's most raw and mature work.

The album included some incredible tracks which, unfortunately, remain rarities as far as Def Leppard tour setlists go: "All I Want Is Everything" featured some of Joe Elliott's best songwriting and vocals; the same can be said about "Where Does Love Go When It Dies" and "Blood Runs Cold" (which Joe co-wrote with Phil Collen). Other standout tracks that still hold their own include "Turn to Dust" and "Pearl of Euphoria."

Whether or not *Slang*'s songs *sound* like Def Leppard is beside the point; most of the tracks are solid and easily stand on their own.

In hindsight, *Slang* could feasibly be interpreted as a concept album, not only representing the challenging music climate of the mid-90s but also as Def Leppard's manifesto to the industry and fans who had dismissed them and moved on. But that's a discussion for another time!

Joe Elliott reflected on the divided response to *Slang* and summed it up this way:

> *"Some people think it's the best thing we ever did, some people think it's the worst thing we ever did."*

As for whether *Slang* is Def Leppard's best or worst album, that's entirely up to you.

In the end, though, it was the right album at the right time.

Album Spotlight: *Euphoria*

Def Leppard's *Euphoria* album was released in June 1999.

The More Things Change, The More They Stay The Same

By 1999, the grunge movement which tormented Def Leppard's brand of music had mostly come and gone.

Feel-good pop songs were not only returning to radio station playlists, but they were also no longer frowned upon by "mainstream" audiences.

What better way for Def Leppard to make the most of this more welcoming environment than put out an album like *Euphoria*!

Like a runaway Mack, like a Union Jack, let's take an in-depth look back at the release.

Back In Your Face Like They've Never Been Away

Euphoria was a return to form for Def Leppard.

It featured the band's trademark hooks, vintage harmonies, a signature polished production, and even resumed the tradition of being a single-worded album title ending in "ia," just like *Pyromania* and *Hysteria*.

Euphoria also featured a bright, colorful album cover (courtesy of *Pyromania* and *Hysteria* album designer Andie Airfix), which literally spotlighted the band's classic logo. This was yet another example of reinforcing the message Def Leppard was trying to get across: We're back!

A 'Promising' Launch

Euphoria had all the makings of a big, commercially successful Def Leppard album.

Even without Robert John "Mutt" Lange to lead the album's production (Pete Woodroffe produced it), Mutt did co-write a few of its songs: "Promises," "It's Only Love," and "All Night."

"Promises," the album's standout track, was an excellent, radio-friendly single that helped reintroduce Def Leppard *and* the band's classic familiar sound to fans.

It was initially promoted as a semi-follow-up to the band's iconic song "Photograph," which wasn't quite fair. Sure, it may very well have been in the *spirit* of Def Leppard's 1983 classic, but "Promises" being the caliber of "Photograph" is another matter entirely.

"Promises" accomplished its task as *Euphoria*'s lead-off single, hitting all the right notes -- figuratively and literally -- and reestablishing the band's presence on radio.

The track reached #1 on *Billboard*'s specialized Mainstream Rock chart, which was better suited for Def Leppard's music at the time, instead of the flagship Hot 100 singles chart, whose top songs that same week included acts such as Jennifer Lopez, TLC, Ricky Martin, Backstreet Boys, and Pearl Jam.

Euphoria Songs, Singles, And Missed Opportunities

Unfortunately, many of *Euphoria*'s strongest tracks were never promoted to radio stations, which could have provided a much larger audience -- especially fans the band lost touch with during the *Slang* years -- the opportunity to rediscover a more vintage Def Leppard.

And therein lies the issue of missed opportunities.

"Promises" kicked things off splendidly, but *Euphoria*'s promotional push quickly dwindled after the single had its run. Several other *rock* tracks worthy of radio station airplay consideration weren't given the chance to follow it up.

"Demolition Man" was an excellent rocker, not to mention an effective opening track for the album. Its fast pace and "Ballroom Blitz"-like chorus could have connected well with rock radio audiences. But it wasn't given a chance.

"Back In Your Face" was in the spirit of arena rocker "Rock and Roll Part II" and did a wonderful job showcasing an assertive sound and attitude that harkened back to the band's *Pyromania* days. But it wasn't given a chance.

"21st Century Sha La La La Girl" lived up to its "*galactic sugar high*" lyric with its frenetic energy, and the song's rap-like verses were reminiscent of "Pour Some Sugar on Me," albeit with a refreshed, late-'90s vibe. But it, too, wasn't given a legitimate chance.

These rock tracks best represented *Euphoria*'s commercial appeal and would have added more heft to the album's overall promotional push.

Releasing them as singles could have also complemented additional *Euphoria* tracks that targeted album-oriented rock (AOR) radio stations: "Paper Sun" fit right in with previous band epics like "Gods of War" and "White Lightning"; "Kings of Oblivion" (which, unlike "Paper Sun," was *not* promoted to AOR stations) conjured up thoughts of an earlier Def Leppard era and should have had the opportunity to connect with listeners. Old-school Def Leppard fans would likely have embraced the song had they heard it.

The point *isn't* that a multitude of *Euphoria* tracks should have been released and given a promotional push because that's not realistic. (Frankly, tracks like "All Night," "Guilty," and "Day After Day" were best suited as deep cuts. As enjoyable as they may be for some, they arguably lack the resilience of many other enduring Def Leppard classics.)

The point *is* a more strategic, cohesive promotional plan might have given *Euphoria* a better, and much longer, opportunity to flourish. The band did its part, touring for well over a year (150+ shows) to support the album. But as for how long *Euphoria* lasted on *Billboard*'s album chart? Only 16 weeks.

The *Euphoria* Ballads

Euphoria doesn't include a "signature" power ballad.

While some may opine that "Goodbye" fits the bill, its unique arrangement and atypical chorus not only make the song an album outlier but also one that is not the type of power ballad Def Leppard fans would expect.

Somewhat surprisingly, "Goodbye" was selected as the album's second U.S. single; furthermore, it was released four *long* months after "Promises." As a result, and not surprising, is that it failed to even chart.

"To Be Alive," another unique *Euphoria* ballad, is a wonderful, yet underrated, song that deserved more attention. Though it wasn't a single, it's arguably more memorable and remembered even more fondly than "Goodbye."

Ballad "It's Only Love" works just fine as an adult contemporary deep track, also foreshadowing the lighter pop sound the band would pursue in future albums *X* and *Songs from the Sparkle Lounge*.

Euphoria Reception

Euphoria debuted at #11 on *Billboard*'s U.S. album chart and ended up being certified gold, on par with *Slang*'s album sales. It's a far cry from the multi-platinum days of *Pyromania*, *Hysteria,* and *Adrenalize*, but still a respectable result for a late-'90s Def Leppard album receiving a limited promotional push.

Decades since its release, fondness for *Euphoria* has mostly grown among fans, as it's recognized for what it is: a Def Leppard album filled with some really good songs!

Euphoria can also be considered a farewell of sorts to Def Leppard's era of big productions and glam-inspired albums -- another reason why it was given a second life, especially for fans who may have missed out on *Euphoria* the first time around, when it was remastered and included in the band's "Vol. 2" deluxe box set release in June 2019. (The album was simultaneously offered on vinyl for the first time, too.)

The Sequel To *Hysteria*?

Not only was *Euphoria* the type of record many Def Leppard fans coveted in 1999, but it also featured the commercial sound and appeal the band's record company was hoping for, so much so that their marketing strategy positioned *Euphoria* as *the sequel* to *Pyromania* and *Hysteria*.

Posters and other P.O.P. (point of purchase) materials created by the record company to promote *Euphoria* at stores actually stated "*After Pyromania and Hysteria comes…Euphoria.*"

Bear in mind that since *Pyromania* and *Hysteria*, the band released original studio albums *Adrenalize* (1992) and *Slang* (1996). But as a promotional strategy, it was decided that *Euphoria* would be the worthy successor to Def Leppard's most successful, commercial-sounding albums. (Having the album's one-word title end with "ia" also helped make the case.)

Whether that's fair to *Adrenalize*, which far outsold *Euphoria*, is debatable. But as a marketing hook intending to reintroduce, position, and brand *Euphoria* (and the band) to the masses, it was an understandable move.

Final Thoughts

After taking a short-term detour with the *Slang* release, *Euphoria* provided Def Leppard the opportunity to revisit the signature sound that turned the band into a superstar act.

Might the album have reached a wider audience and been more commercially successful had it had a longer-term, strategic promotional push? Arguably, yes. Nevertheless, the message *Euphoria* conveyed was still abundantly clear: Def Leppard was back!

And while *Euphoria* rewarded fans who endured the dark days of grunge in the '90s and longed for vintage Def Leppard, the album *still* rewards and warrants repeated listens.

Album Spotlight: X

Def Leppard's *X* album was released in July 2002.

There is a long, long way to go with this in-depth look back at the album, as it will also discuss the challenging circumstances surrounding the *X* release and the missed opportunities that ultimately led to its commercial underperformance.

X Marks What Spot?

Def Leppard's *X* (the Roman numeral for "10," to commemorate their tenth studio album release) most likely divides the band's fanbase into three different groups:

> 1. Fans who love any new music Def Leppard releases, regardless of whether it "rocks hard" or not.
>
> 2. Fans who appreciate a new Def Leppard album but admit they sometimes miss their mark, yet don't fault the band for trying something different.
>
> 3. Fans who feel let down and disappointed when a new Def Leppard album (a) doesn't sound like *On Through The Night* or *High 'n' Dry*, (b) doesn't sound like *Pyromania* or *Hysteria*, or (c) features songs that sound way too poppy or border on adult contemporary.

Any one of those three groups has its fair share of supporters.

As mentioned in other album spotlights in this book (like the ones for *Adrenalize* and *Slang*), it's important to keep in mind the state of the music industry -- and Def Leppard's place in it -- when *X* was released.

The year was 2002. It had been three years since *Euphoria*, an album recorded and positioned in the same vein as *Hysteria*. (The band's record company went so far as to label *Euphoria* the final piece in Def Leppard's trilogy of massive album productions, the successor to *Pyromania* and *Hysteria*, overlooking *Adrenalize* altogether.)

So what was the band to do now? Venture into a different musical direction again and release another *Slang*-like album, which likely meant sacrificing commercial viability? Or maybe attempt something more raw and hard rock, harkening back to an earlier Def Leppard era?

Recording another album like *Adrenalize* or *Euphoria* was an option, too, but the band wasn't interested in revamping previous efforts.

During an interview discussing *Euphoria*, Phil Collen told Billboard.com the band would sometimes "borrow" from their own work to create new songs that were similar to previous Def Leppard hits:

> "We desperately tried to do that," he says with a laugh. "With 'Promises,' I made the riff in the same key as 'Armageddon It' and 'Photograph.' It's basically a rip-off. If another band was to do that to us, we'd go 'Jesus Christ, let's sue them.' But no one noticed."

He went on to also explain how *X* differed from *Euphoria* and other previous Def Leppard albums:

> "On this record ['X'], we didn't do that at all. This record

was quite liberating. We weren't sticking to any rigid walls or boundaries, which were done on pretty much all of the other records."

Phil's comment could also apply to future albums *Songs from the Sparkle Lounge* and the band's self-titled *Def Leppard*, maybe even more so. Because while *X* was "liberating" in its own right, external factors beyond the band's control constrained and impeded its commercial fate.

Do You Wanna Get... *X*'ed?

Going with another *Adrenalize* or *Euphoria*-type album would not have worked very well in 2002. The music industry was still in flux, and the band was no longer the radio and chart powerhouse it used to be.

For instance, the week *X* debuted on *Billboard*'s album chart, top positions were held by Bruce Springsteen, Nelly, Linkin Park, Eminem, Avril Lavigne, and so on; the days of battling acts like Guns N' Roses, Van Halen, and Poison for chart dominance were a distant memory.

So for Def Leppard to return to the public eye with a song like "Let's Get Rocked" or "Make Love Like A Man" may have satisfied some fans, but it also would have done some damage to the band's brand, creatively and commercially.

The band was at a crossroads and ultimately decided to try some different things which resulted in a more "mature" sounding Def Leppard album, one that also included songs written by outside songwriters.

To think that Def Leppard would relinquish songwriting duties to outsiders who wrote songs for acts such as Britney Spears and Backstreet Boys (and Nicki Minaj and One Direction thereafter) was hard to fathom.

In recent years, Joe Elliott shared how he initially responded to the suggestion of bringing in outside songwriters for the *X* album:

> "I was completely not cool with [outside writers], cause I knew that we were well capable of writing [songs] on our own, so why would we want to do that?"

This shows the lack of faith external forces had in the band in the early 2000s, as the insinuation was clear: Def Leppard was no longer capable of putting out a successful album of hit songs on their own.

Even though Joe took a more diplomatic route regarding the matter, saying the band considered outside songwriters more of an "experiment," and that the resulting songs were in the spirit of one of his favorite bands, Cheap Trick, the way he ended his point was telling:

> "I think the stuff we wrote on our own has the real flavor of what Def Leppard is."

Ironically, none of the tracks written by or with outside songwriters resulted in a "hit" song for the *X* album. To be fair, those so-called "experiments" didn't adversely hurt the album either; actually, some of them resulted in songs that were worthy additions to the band's catalog.

Def Leppard's *X* album did indeed have something working against it, though, that hurt its chances of commercial success: a release strategy that lacked...a release strategy.

X Release Strategy, Or Lack Thereof

The band's record company released "Now" as *X*'s first single, along with a fairly amusing music video whose storyline centered around the decades-long journey of a vintage Def Leppard Union Jack shirt, which was intermixed with the band's performance of the song.

On the surface (and putting aside the overdone acting in the storyline portion), the video tells a "fun" tale as the Union Jack shirt is disregarded and misplaced over the years, going through its share of owners, and finally resurfacing when it's purchased on an online auction by the person who owned it originally.

Giving this concept the benefit of the doubt, you *could* assume the music video was conveying how Def Leppard's appeal crosses generations.

Beneath the surface, though, the video seemed to depict Def Leppard's iconic "Union Jack" era (aka the *Pyromania* era) as a novelty, hokey, a relic of the past, and something that was no longer a fundamental part of the band.

Moreover, not only did it seem to portray Def Leppard as a band that was no longer in its heyday but also as one that had willingly moved on from it, basically telling viewers and long-time fans: *"We've grown up and matured since those silly Union Jack years. We should be taken more seriously now."*

Arguably, the "Now" video diminished Def Leppard's image by trying to reposition and market the band as more "current" with the times.

Not Right "Now"

"Now" is a good, rather straightforward, song. Its verses are effective in their delivery, and momentum builds quite nicely to the chorus which, for better or worse, is somewhat un-Leppard-like.

That aside, "Now" is better off residing and thriving as an appealing deep track; it does not have, nor did it ever have, the makings of a chart-conquering hit single, especially one that would dominate radio playlists and handle the important task of launching an album.

Again, *X* marked the return of Def Leppard after a *three-year-long* hiatus; "Now" wasn't powerful enough to reintroduce the band back onto the airwaves and reconnect them with listeners and casual fans.

The band's record company must have realized this, too, as they decided to not go the route of a typical single release, instead choosing to *only* target rock radio stations with "Now."

So right off the bat, a small-scale approach.

How did that work out? "Now" didn't even crack the Top 25 on *Billboard*'s niche Mainstream Rock Tracks chart; it also barely made it onto *Billboard*'s Adult Contemporary chart, which could be considered a positive and negative -- after all, should the *first* "single" off of a new Def Leppard album be an adult contemporary success?

From an industry and chart perspective, "Now" was over (figuratively speaking) before it even began. So much for making a meaningful impact to launch a brand new Def Leppard album.

Even More Missteps

After "Now" quickly fizzled out -- which, consequently, didn't create crucial album sales momentum to coincide with Def Leppard's *X* tour -- it appeared as if the band's record company had already determined *X* would not be a hit.

The band's excellent rocker "Four Letter Word" ended up being more of a throwaway track to AOR (album-oriented rock) radio stations *months* after "Now" had come and gone, and it lacked any type of significant promotional push.

As a result, "Four Letter Word" barely made a blip, even underperforming "Now" on *Billboard*'s Mainstream Rock chart.

Def Leppard did its part, though, even performing "Four Letter Word" on the *X* tour, but without radio support to help drive awareness (and album sales), the track soon disappeared from the band's setlist.

A last-ditch Hail Mary effort was attempted long after *X* debuted and disappeared from the album chart: the band's moody ballad "Long Long Way To Go" was released...*nine months* after *X* came out.

At such a late stage, "Long Long Way To Go" was more of an after-thought; unsurprisingly, it quickly came and went, just like the *X* album.

Similar to *Euphoria*, *X* debuted just outside of the Top 10 on *Billboard*'s U.S. album chart, at #11. Whereas an album typically has its peaks and valleys on the chart, driven by radio, marketing, and tour support, the lack of those components working together cohesively is emblematic of *X*'s chart lifespan: 8 very short weeks.

X's weekly album chart positions in the U.S. can be summed up ever-so-briefly: #11 (debut week), #36, #73, #88, #122, #129, #147, #167, and then gone. Poof. Done.

X didn't even reach gold certification status.

X Could Have Marked The Spot Better

What's most disappointing about Def Leppard's *X* sales performance is that it didn't have to be that way. The album could have had a much more effective launch and long-term promotional push.

As the band stated at the time, *X* showcased their "many flavors"; unfortunately, that message never came across or reached the masses.

A comprehensive, multi-format radio campaign could have been more effective, one that promoted various songs off the album to different radio audiences.

For example:

- **"Unbelievable"** was radio-friendly and readymade for Top 40 and Adult Contemporary stations (even though this is one of the songs the band didn't write, it's a solid track);
- **"Everyday"** was perfectly suited for AOR stations, and remains one of Def Leppard's best album cuts;
- **"Torn to Shreds"** deserved single consideration, featuring some of the best hooks and harmonies the band has ever recorded;
- **"Four Letter Word"** harkened back to the band's *High 'n' Dry* era and would have made a greater impact on rock stations had its release been timed better, as part of a long-term radio promotion strategy.

There's no reason why multiple radio formats couldn't have been simultaneously targeted with different *X* tracks. It's not a new idea, and it could have effectively provided Def Leppard with airplay coverage on stations across the country, raised awareness of the band's return, and, most importantly, provided sustainable sales momentum for the *X* album.

"Long Long Way To Go" *then* could have been released as a single, as it would have been optimally timed and based on how the previous radio releases were performing.

Put simply, a more strategic plan should have been developed and implemented, giving *X* a fighting chance to succeed. Alas, none of that was to be.

X Could Have Been... *X*-Ier

For those not aware, the *X* album introduced a good, yet

mostly overlooked, B-side titled "10X Bigger Than Love."

The track brings to mind the days of *Hysteria*, when Def Leppard's B-sides were not only worthy of album inclusion but sometimes better than some of the tracks that made the final cut. That being said, this hard-rocking, catchy song (along with its standout guitar solo) would have added more heft to *X*, and would have been a fitting counterpart to "Four Letter Word."

Separately, *X* also has its shortfalls:

- **"Let Me Be The One"** would have worked better if the band went with their demo's original piano-driven version instead, which was more melodic and compelling;

- **"Perfect Girl"** is the original -- and, arguably, superior -- version to album track **"Gravity,"** and it would have been a better, more memorable fit for *X*;

- **"You're So Beautiful"** becomes too hook-driven for its own good, layering hook upon hook...upon yet another hook, which ends up working against it. (The hook overcompensation seems to fit the narrative of external involvement as well as self-inflicted pressure to make sure the album contained its share of "hit songs.")

That aside, there was a lot of material to work with on *X*. Unfortunately, numerous avenues that were potentially rewarding weren't pursued. Hence, it's not all that surprising that *X*'s commercial success suffered. (It's also not a coincidence that the band ended up breaking away from their record company years later, after fulfilling their contractual album obligations.)

X Is Worth Revisiting

It's easy to dismiss *X*'s poor sales performance and blame its pop-lite offerings as the main cause, but that would require overlooking the song gems that resided on the album.

The album wasn't given a proper chance to shine, or at least garner the attention it deserved; the same can be said about the band at the time. Fortunately, they began taking more control of Def Leppard's proverbial reins going forward, no longer letting outside influences guide -- better yet, misguide -- them.

Final Thoughts

Was *X* destined to reach the same commercial heights as Def Leppard's biggest albums? No, that's unrealistic.

Were there numerous missed opportunities in how *X* was positioned and promoted? Absolutely.

In recent years, Joe Elliott summed up the *X* album this way:

> *"It's not a standout album. I don't think it's a complete duffer [slang for ineffectual, worthless], and it's certainly not 'Hysteria.' But there is some cool stuff on it."*

If only more people had the chance to discover all that cool stuff when it was released.

Album Spotlight: Songs From The Sparkle Lounge

Def Leppard's *Songs from the Sparkle Lounge* was released in April 2008 and marked the band's return after a six-year-long hiatus between original studio albums. During that time, they primarily kept themselves busy recording their *Yeah!* covers album release and relentless touring.

The album is aptly titled, referencing the backstage area the band utilized during their 2007 tour to develop its collection of songs.

Joe Elliott explained how the unique "sparkle lounge" setting came about to Billboard.com:

> "The crew started having a bit of fun with it, putting in sparkly lights, candles, incense -- you name it. It turned into this very atmospheric little workspace."

Welcome To The *Sparkle Lounge*

Clocking in at just under 40 minutes, *Songs from the Sparkle Lounge* featured an assortment of notably short, pop-leaning tracks not unlike Def Leppard's previous album *X*, albeit with a slightly harder edge.

The album's songwriting approach was also vastly different than most of the band's previous releases; for the most part, songs were written by only one band member this time around.

Aside from opening track "Go" (written by Joe Elliott and Phil Collen) and "Nine Lives" (written by Joe, Phil, Rick Savage, and Tim McGraw), the album's nine remaining tracks had only one songwriting credit:

- "Go" (Collen, Elliott)
- "Nine Lives" (Collen, Elliott, McGraw, Savage)
- "C'mon C'mon" (Savage)
- "Love" (Savage)
- "Tomorrow" (Collen)
- "Cruise Control" (Campbell)
- "Hallucinate" (Collen)
- "Only the Good Die Young" (Campbell)
- "Bad Actress" (Elliott)
- "Come Undone" (Elliott)
- "Gotta Let It Go" (Campbell)

Even without knowing who officially wrote which track, it's fairly easy to identify the band member behind each song: melody-infused tracks "C'mon C'mon" and "Love" had Rick Savage's glam-rock influenced signature all over them; Joe Elliott's "Come Undone" and "Bad Actress" showcased his distinct, harder-edged song approach ("Bad Actress" also resembled the *Adrenalize* era B-side "She's Too Tough," which Joe also wrote); Phil Collen's unmistakable guitar-driven arrangements were on full display on "Tomorrow" and "Hallucinate" (in hindsight, the latter song sounds like a precursor to *Mirror Ball*'s "It's All About Believing," which Phil also penned); Vivian Campbell's blues and psychedelic music influences came across loud and clear on tracks "Cruise Control," "Only The Good Die Young," and "Gotta Let It Go," all of which he wrote.

Having only one band member receive songwriting credit shouldn't be that surprising, as the technological times -- and the band's recording process -- had evolved, especially when compared to earlier Def Leppard releases. The band was no longer cooped up in a recording studio for extended periods solely focused on creating an album together. And unlike *X*, outside songwriters weren't brought in to contribute either.

Instead, each band member was able to work on song concepts at their own pace while on tour, and then bring those ideas to the "sparkle lounge" for group consideration and validation, giving true meaning to the phrase "songs from the sparkle lounge."

Does this mean the album is disjointed or lacks cohesion as a band effort since it's mostly comprised of individual song contributions? Not necessarily.

Songs from the Sparkle Lounge ultimately showcased various facets of the band and spotlighted a freestyle approach that would be taken even further on their self-titled *Def Leppard* album.

Sometimes You Win, Sometimes You Lose

Songs from the Sparkle Lounge had a very respectable Top 5 album debut in the U.S., selling approximately 55,000 units in its first week. (It was a Top 10 album in the U.K.)

Lead single "Nine Lives" brought additional notoriety as a result of Def Leppard's collaboration with Tim McGraw, but there was also a trade-off: some fans weren't exactly thrilled about the band veering into country music territory.

Teaming up with a country superstar like McGraw undoubtedly increased awareness of the album and helped introduce Def Leppard to a broader audience, but it was still risky making "Nine Lives" the *first* single; it was a unique track that didn't quite represent *Songs from the Sparkle Lounge*, and it wasn't the most radio-friendly song to handle the crucial role of launching the album, not to mention reconnect Def Leppard with longtime fans.

"Nine Lives" certainly garnered attention early on, but that initial interest and curiosity was arguably more about the rock and country music collaboration and not necessarily about the song itself. Accordingly, the "Nine Lives" single didn't even make it onto *Billboard*'s Hot 100 singles chart.

The chart life of a Def Leppard album released in 2008 was unquestionably going to be shorter than *Pyromania*, *Hysteria*, and even *Adrenalize*. It was just a question of how much shorter it would be and what could be done to prolong its duration. By the time "C'mon C'mon" was released as the album's second single *nearly three months* after "Nine Lives," *Songs from the Sparkle Lounge*'s sales momentum was practically non-existent. The album ended up lasting on *Billboard*'s album chart for eight very brief weeks, never to return.

Might there have been a better strategy to market and promote the album? Potentially.

A more focused, strategic approach could arguably have made a difference, including going with arena-rocker "C'mon C'mon" as the first single, utilizing "Go" and "Tomorrow" for targeting album-oriented rock (AOR) radio stations, giving ballad "Love" a chance as a single, and so on.

"Nine Lives" still could have had its own single release at some point, just not as the launching pad for the album.

Unfortunately, "Nine Lives" was chosen to not only hype but more or less carry the album, which was impractical. That being said, sales for *Songs from the Sparkle Lounge* failed to even reach gold status.

Final Thoughts

Songs from the Sparkle Lounge isn't likely at the very top of many fans' lists of favorite Def Leppard albums. Nevertheless, the release provided an opportunity for the band to exercise its creative muscle, churn out new music (for themselves and longing fans), and return to touring with some fresh new songs in hand.

The album's standout tracks still resonate -- most notably "C'mon C'mon," guitar-driven rocker "Go," underrated gem "Tomorrow," and the Queen-esque, emotionally charged ballad "Love."

In the end, new music from the band will always be welcomed. And just because *Songs from the Sparkle Lounge* doesn't always shine for some doesn't mean Def Leppard's sparkle has lost any of its luster.

Album Spotlight: Def Leppard

    The self-titled *Def Leppard* album was released in October 2015, seven years after the band's previous effort *Songs from the Sparkle Lounge*.

    The length of time between the two projects was understandable. After all, the critical importance of releasing a new album wasn't what it used to be, not by a long shot. What was once considered a necessity, and an essential tool to plan a tour around, had become increasingly irrelevant, especially at this point in the band's career.

    Many of the traditional components (and benefits) typically associated with a new music project had fundamentally and forever changed. As a result, the prioritization and urgency for a new album had, too, ultimately leading Def Leppard to change its approach to releasing new music.

    This deep dive will go further into this topic and so much more.

    Do you really, really wanna do this now? If so, prepare to take an in-depth look back at Def Leppard's self-titled *Def Leppard* album.

"Let's Go" A Different Route

    By 2015, Def Leppard was in a different career mindset.

The band was no longer contractually obligated to release a number of albums on behalf of a record label over a specified period of time. Moreover, the days of feeling any pressure whatsoever to outdo previous monster album releases -- production-wise, sales-wise, or tour-wise -- were long gone, too.

From a creative and business standpoint, this afforded the band more freedom and flexibility in determining what direction they wanted to go in, and where to place their focus. This additional control was not only better for the band, but it also made a lot more sense, as so much had changed in the music industry over the years.

During the days of *Pyromania*, *Hysteria*, *Adrenalize*, and to an extent, *Euphoria*, comprehensive promotional strategies were put into place to launch and market those albums. But by 2015, many of those sales and marketing initiatives didn't matter, some didn't even exist anymore.

For instance, how many singles will there be from the album? How will the releases be timed? Will there be a multi-format radio strategy (i.e., will some tracks solely target specific radio station formats like album-oriented rock stations, adult contemporary stations, etc.)? Which ones will be official singles to target mainstream Top 40 radio stations? And so on.

Frankly, those types of questions didn't apply to Def Leppard. Even the word "single" had lost its meaning.

As had been the case for years, having a Def Leppard song soar up *Billboard*'s Hot 100 singles chart, let alone sit atop it, wasn't a priority nor a realistic expectation. That's not to say the band wasn't putting out quality songs; it's just that the industry and radio landscape had changed significantly.

Way back when, a Def Leppard hit song occupying *Billboard*'s Hot 100 singles chart involved the culmination of heavy national radio airplay (no longer the case by 2015), considerable MTV support (the network perceived as a promotional outlet was a distant memory), substantial single sales (the days of cassingles and CD-singles being purchased in mass were long gone), and so on.

Singles lost their impact and inevitably became less rewarding, hence less worth the time, effort, and expense.

The same increasingly applied to albums. Case in point, remember going into a record store weeks before a major album release? P.O.P. (point-of-purchase) materials such as posters and flyers would decorate sections of the store, hyping the event. Cashier areas would have bag stuffers reminding customers of the upcoming album's release date; select, high-profile locations would even have contest entry boxes to win a copy of the album or win tickets to the artist's local tour date.

Upon the album's release, you couldn't miss its availability when shopping those stores; updated signage would adorn the walls and windows, and album copies would fill shelves and racks, just waiting for consumers to nab them.

Most of these types of record stores were gone by 2015. And while few remained, even major chains like Best Buy weren't avid supporters of the CD format anymore, requiring consumers to flip through alphabetized bins just to try and find a few copies of an album the store *might* be offering.

In short, a new album -- more specifically, sales from a new album -- wasn't as consequential and didn't provide anywhere near the revenue stream it used to. (While vinyl has become a nice little sales niche in recent years, it remains just that, a niche.)

With the realization that numerous traditional sales outlets and promotional options were extremely limited, and knowing the majority of consumers were not even purchasing complete albums -- instead, in the age of digital, many preferred to stream or simply select the tracks they wanted to own -- a full-length release imminently decreased in importance.

So if or when Def Leppard were to put out an album, the majority of what used to be a tried and true release strategy --

from marketing to radio to retail sales -- has been turned on its head. As a result, Def Leppard adapted, re-prioritized, and altered their overall approach.

"We Belong" On The Road

A seven-year gap between albums is a long time, but that doesn't mean the band was out of the spotlight. Their main focus and priority between the two projects can primarily be summed up in one word: touring.

The days of Def Leppard vanishing from the public eye and locking themselves in a studio to feverishly work on an album, only to reappear years later to promote it, were gone. Instead, as was done for years prior to the *Def Leppard* release, the band toured. And toured. And toured. Without any new original studio album to promote.

Previous album *Songs from the Sparkle Lounge* put the band on the road for most of 2008 and 2009. After that? More touring!

- 2011: Toured a good portion of the year around their live release *Mirror Ball*;
- 2012: Performed nearly 50 dates in support of their *Rock of Ages* tour;
- 2013: An international summer tour, followed by their "Viva! Hysteria" Las Vegas residency;
- 2014: Summer tour with KISS (42 tour dates)

The band certainly kept itself busy, and to the delight of concertgoers, toured extensively *every year* between the release of *Songs from the Sparkle Lounge* and *Def Leppard*.

In recent years, Joe Elliott addressed the topic of recording new music versus touring, reiterating Def Leppard's priority:

"Playing live is, at this moment in time, more important

than new music."

Do You Really, Really Wanna...Record A New Album?

The *Def Leppard* album was not part of the band's original plan.

Initially, the intention was to record a few new songs, potentially release them as an EP, and then go back on tour. So many new song ideas developed in the process though that -- voila! -- a new Def Leppard album emerged.

In a broader sense, the band continuing to have the creative drive to write new music benefits themselves as well as fans. In addition, their approach to making a new album is emblematic of Def Leppard at this point in its career: they have the luxury of recording new music only when the need and desire arise. The band is now well-established, has a locked-in fanbase, and has mastered the art of putting on a great live show.

From a business perspective, touring relentlessly continues to be the most pragmatic route, as it's truly the most stable and lucrative income stream for the band (pre- and post-pandemic).

Nevertheless, new music will always attract added attention since it's become a rarity, and that it's done because the band *wants* to do it, not because they *have* to.

Which brings us to the self-titled *Def Leppard* album.

Def Leppard Meets *Def Leppard*

Recall if you will when outside songwriters were brought in to supply the band with songs for the *X* album. Or the time when the band felt the pressures of coming up with yet another commercially successful album (which became *Adrenalize*) in hopes of repeating previous monster sales feats.

Those types of scenarios and distractions seemed ancient by 2015.

The band no longer felt constrained or obligated to abide by other peoples' wishes or timelines, which makes the *Def Leppard* album more unique than all of their previous efforts. It's unrestricted, with music and artistic expression at its core, as epitomized on the *Def Leppard* album cover which features the band's classic logo shattering through a glass wall.

Vivian Campbell touched on why the band still feels the need to exercise its creative artistry:

> *"I think there's a few things that keep bands vital. For Def Leppard, one of those things is that we continue to occasionally make new albums...even though some people say, 'Why do you even bother? People just wanna hear your hits. You do very good business by just going out and playing your hit songs.' But it's important for the lifeblood of Def Leppard as a band that we continue to be a creative unit."*

It's that mindset that resulted in *Def Leppard*, fourteen tracks showcasing the band flexing its creative muscles -- all the more reason the album's title is fitting: it's *their* album, on *their* terms, done *their* way.

Def Leppard is the band's most diverse album. It does not harken back to any particular Def Leppard era, but there are instances where a song will conjure up thoughts of a previous Def Leppard hit.

The Tracklisting

Most songs on the *Def Leppard* album were written by one

or two band members. Here's a breakdown of the tracklisting along with who wrote each song:

- "Let's Go" (Rick Savage, Joe Elliott)
- "Dangerous" (Phil Collen, Joe Elliott)
- "Man Enough" (Phil Collen, Joe Elliott)
- "We Belong" (Joe Elliott)
- "Invincible" (Rick Allen, Joe Elliott)
- "Sea of Love" (Phil Collen)
- "Energized" (Phil Collen)
- "All Time High" (Joe Elliott)
- "Battle of My Own" (Rick Savage, Joe Elliott)
- "Broke 'N' Brokenhearted" (Phil Collen, Joe Elliott)
- "Forever Young" (Phil Collen, Joe Elliott)
- "Last Dance" (Rick Savage)
- "Wings of an Angel" (Phil Collen, Vivian Campbell, Rick Savage, Joe Elliott)
- "Blind Faith" (Phil Collen, Vivian Campbell, Rick Savage, Joe Elliott)

The album provided the opportunity for the band to experiment freely and go down numerous musical paths, some of which they'd never done before.

It's quite an eclectic listening experience: Delve into Beatlesque territory with "Blind Faith"; enjoy a blend of folk music, blues, and a dose of Led Zeppelin with "Battle of My Own"; take a ride with the band flat-out jamming with their raw, attitude-filled "Forever Young." And that's just the tip of the proverbial iceberg.

The "Singles"

Several tracks were utilized to promote the *Def Leppard*

album.

First was "Let's Go," a guitar-driven track intentionally made to sound exactly like the type of song Def Leppard fans would expect. It's no surprise it was chosen to launch the album, as it unapologetically puts the band's signature sound on full display.

Joe Elliott spoke to Rolling Stone about the song:

> *"It has that swaggering, mid-tempo rhythm, like 'Sugar,' and 'Rock of Ages.' The idea was, we wanted something familiar."*

"Dangerous," another track that leaned towards a sound from an earlier Def Leppard era, followed it up.

Next was "Man Enough," with its prominent "Another One Bites The Dust"-like bass line groove.

And, finally, "We Belong," the album's standout track, featuring each band member taking turns singing lead vocals.

These four tracks were positioned as the *Def Leppard* album's "singles," but they could just as easily have been referred to as promotional tracks, as single chart performance hadn't been relevant for a very long time.

The Music Videos

Music videos were created for the album's four promotional tracks, with each one showcasing a sci-fi animation storyline interspersed (in some shape or form) with band performance footage.

Did these music videos enhance the songs and upsell them? Frankly, not really.

The videos would have been more effective and memorable if they focused (much) less on the obscure and rather distracting sci-fi animation and (much) more on the band members themselves.

Think back to the music videos for "Photograph" or "Pour Some Sugar On Me" or "Let's Get Rocked," and so on: those unforgettable visual experiences are embedded in fans' minds, forever conjoined to the songs they represent.

Unfortunately, the four music videos from the *Def Leppard* album all mix together, mostly lacking any of their own identifiable traits.

Final Thoughts

Def Leppard debuted at a very respectable #10 on *Billboard*'s U.S. top albums chart, thanks in part to the band resolving their long-standing digital rights dispute with their record company which allowed them to also offer the album digitally.

The album was the band's seventh Top 10 U.S. album release, an impressive achievement, especially for a band that was approaching its fourth decade in existence.

Even though Vivian Campbell's album contributions were limited due to ongoing health issues, he went on to say he believed it was the best album Def Leppard had put out since his time with the band.

Vivian told Cryptic Rock in 2016:

> "I can honestly say I think it's the best record that Def Leppard has put out in the twenty-four years I've been with the band. The irony is, it's the record that I've had the least involvement with. I don't know what that tells me (laughs). The good news is, it is the strongest record [in] many decades from Def Leppard. We are all very proud of that."

During an interview with Boston radio station WAAF, Phil Collen made the following proclamation about the album:

> "I think it's the best thing we've done since 'Hysteria.' I really do."

Undoubtedly, some fans will agree with Phil's opinion, while many others won't.

This brings us right back to where this deep dive began: Up against a music industry environment that had completely changed since the days of *Pyromania* and *Hysteria*, Def Leppard took matters into its own hands and course-corrected, making the most of the situation.

Phil succinctly summed things up this way:

> "There wasn't any industry—no record company executive or anyone—saying, 'You've got to do an album.' It was purely because we wanted to write songs, and we felt the need to do that."

Simply put, the *Def Leppard* album showcases what the band is best at: being Def Leppard.

Would you *really, really* want it any other way?

Personal Story: If It Pleases You, It Pleases...Them

One of the things I find so interesting about a Def Leppard concert, then and now, is how some of their songs, whether new or old, crackle with a whole new level of energy when performed live.

One example is "Armageddon It," no doubt a classic track from the *Hysteria* album, but there's just something about that particular song that (further) comes to life in concert, giving it a spark and making it more lively.

Part of this can be attributed to a pick up in the song's tempo, but ultimately the credit goes to everyone backing up Joe Elliott's lead vocals: Sav's driving bass is even more distinct; Rick's drums more prominent; Phil and Vivian's (and, previously, Steve Clark's) soaring guitars sounding even more robust.

It all works together seamlessly, further enriched by the band's magnificent live backing vocals. There's just an overall verve and raw vibe which amplifies the album version many know and love.

Am I reading too much into this? Possibly. But in the end, I think most Def Leppard fans would agree that when "Armageddon It" is performed live, the concert's momentum really picks up and takes on a party-like atmosphere.

I believe the same can be said about the song "Slang," a track that didn't get much traction in the U.S. but was still performed live by the band on numerous occasions in support of the *Slang* album.

The times I saw Def Leppard perform the song on tour in the '90s, I was always taken aback by how well it went over with crowds. (The song would resurface again, as recently as the band's 2019 Las Vegas residency at the Zappos Theater, and again was a hit with audiences.)

Of all the songs on the band's setlist during the *Slang* tour, "Slang" was the one I went out of my way to mention to Joe when I had the opportunity to chat with him at a show's after-party. Not that my opinion made any difference, but I made sure to call out the newfound energy I felt they brought to it with their performance, and most especially how well-received it was by the audience.

Joe appreciated the compliment and seemed to have a genuine interest in hearing the "critique" about their performance. These types of casual conversations typically ended with Joe humbly responding with, "Thank you very much," which brings to mind a related discussion I had with a coworker at the record label who was also a close, personal friend of the band.

He had overheard my discussion with Joe and pointed out something I still remember to this day.

He told me, "When a concert audience isn't being responsive to the band's performance, the band *never* blames the audience for having an 'off night.'" He continued, "They blame themselves. That's just how they are."

That always stuck with me.

It says a lot about the band, and the responsibility and pride they take in the shows they put on for fans who spend their hard-earned money to see them. And while this may not be all that surprising, it's a testament to the character and professionalism of the band and its members.

Personal Story: An 'Ugly' Situation With A Concert On The Side

As fans can attest, Def Leppard's live shows provide plenty of special moments and memories; I'm sure anyone who has attended a show has an unforgettable tale to tell.

One such event I will never forget occurred in August 1993 while backstage before a show in Tinley Park, Illinois. The venue was called the World Music Theatre at the time.

There was the "usual" pre-show electricity in the air, where you can practically *feel* the anticipation building, as the buzzing from concert attendees in the distance entering the venue would grow louder with each passing minute.

But this time around, something was different -- and *not* in a good way. There was unusual scurrying going on by some record company personnel whose faces were flashing concerned looks, as well as intense side discussions.

It was quite odd, as I hadn't even had a chance to ask what was going on yet, but it all seemed peculiar, especially since it was still early in the evening and opening act Ugly Kid Joe hadn't even gone on stage yet.

"What's going on?" I asked my coworker.

"Ugly Kid Joe's not going to make it," I was told.

"Not going to make what...the show?" I responded, baffled, as it was so close to showtime.

But that was indeed the case.

Opening act Ugly Kid Joe all of a sudden was no longer going to be...the opening act.

It was unclear at the time, as there were conflicting stories about lead singer Whitfield Crane getting into trouble, potentially at the airport when trying to come into town, that resulted in him missing his flight. Keep in mind, these were the days before readily accessible Blackberry devices or smartphones; communication, especially in the venue's backstage area, relied on landlines -- and that's *if* you were able to get a hold of the person you were trying to locate. (Texting "Where are you?!" wasn't a convenient option.)

After some hurried discussions, and seeing people reach out to contacts who may know other contacts, a Plan B option quickly came together. The convenience of the venue's location worked out perfectly: ask members of Enuff Z'Nuff -- a Chicago-based glam rock band, best known for their ballad "Fly High Michelle" (among other underrated, power pop treats like "Right By Your Side" and "Mother's Eyes") -- if they were available (immediately) to perform.

Band members Chip Z'Nuff and Donnie Vie were able to rush to the venue to take Ugly Kid Joe's slot. (I still recall seeing Chip Z'Nuff dash into the backstage area, guitar case in hand.) No drummer, no show preparation, nothing. Just the two of them sitting on stage with acoustic guitars.

Crisis averted! Especially under the circumstances, it worked out quite well -- Enuff Z'Nuff (Chip and Donnie) put on a solid show for the crowd.

Due to the evening's unique situation and last-minute backstage drama, I ended up watching the opening act entertainment while standing on the side of the stage, which offered a remarkable perspective.

For this particular concert, my allotted ticket was in the front row (after all, it was a Def Leppard show!), but after watching Enuff Z'Nuff's portion, I realized I had never truly watched a Def Leppard concert from the side of the stage, to also see all the goings-on of the stage show from behind the scenes.

Utilizing my All-Access pass, I decided this tour date was as good as any and ended up watching the majority of the show from "stage right."

I peered around the stage side's corner curtain every so often to see the thousands of cheering fans having a great time; it provided an amazingly different perspective and point of view.

For example, it was a treat to see band members leave the stage for a break (i.e., go out of the audience's view), and see where they go and what they do.

One memorable moment was during the band's performance of "Rocket." During this tour, the song's middle section was extended, with Rick Allen's drumming complemented by Joe Elliott's vocal of "Ahh-ahh-ahh...ahh-ahh-ahh-ahhhhh," a melody which would then be countered by Phil and Vivian's guitar playing.

I'd seen this live version of the song performed numerous times previously from a venue's seating area. But from that audience point of view, Joe is not seen on stage, only his voice is heard.

This is another reason why I found this particular performance so unique. While standing on the side of the stage, I got to see Joe disappear from the audience's view and go behind the stage to a designated area where a table with a makeshift, lighted, vanity-like mirror awaited.

Joe would put the microphone down, towel off, take a drink, pick up the microphone, perform the aforementioned "Ahh-ahh-ahh...," put the mic down again, put some eye drops in, take another quick drink, and head back out in front of the audience, never missing a beat.

This is just one example of how unique it was to witness Def Leppard's show this way.

I did go to the seating area for a short time to get an alternate view of things, but ended up going back to watch the majority of the rest of the show from the "sidelines."

It was a one-of-a-kind experience that capped off an unforgettable evening...for multiple reasons!

Personal Story: Definitely Not A Wardrobe Malfunction

If you followed Def Leppard in the mid-'90s, you're likely aware that the band toured outdoor amphitheaters. This was quite a change of pace from their unique, massive "in-the-round" shows, which the band performed during their *Hysteria* tour, and revisited for a portion of the *Adrenalize* tour.

This tour had a distinctly different look and feel. Things were more simplified and modest, from the theatrics of the show to the band itself; even their concert attire was minimal, with denim shorts and an (optional) shirt being the go-to outfit. (The band has jokingly referred to this period as "the wilderness years," which showcased a more laid-back, rugged Def Leppard.)

During one of these "shed" tour shows, I left the backstage space (which was outdoors, too) and went to the venue's seating area to take a couple of snapshots of the concert and partake in the communal audience experience.

Going through a couple of my pictures from this show spurred another special memory.

As you can see in the picture above, Joe Elliott's outfit was very straightforward: jean shorts and a white t-shirt, which included a message on it. The quality of the picture is fairly poor -- darn camera! -- but the story behind it is what makes it so memorable, and it has nothing to do with the song being performed or the concert itself.

Earlier in the day, hours before the show, the backstage area -- again, which was outside due to the venue -- was populated with people preparing for the evening's events (and enjoying a beautiful summer day).

At one point, while I was talking with others, I noticed Joe walk by out of the corner of my eye with a white t-shirt in hand. His other hand held a can of spray paint. He then proceeded to lay the shirt flat on the concrete pavement, bend down and point the spray paint can at it, and spell out the letters of a word.

I couldn't see what Joe had sprayed onto the shirt, but I

found it so amusing hours later when the band appeared on stage: Joe was wearing the white t-shirt with the spray-painted words "DO ME" on it.

It was a treat seeing the shirt's behind-the-scenes "creative design" happen in real-time, from idea to execution.

On a broader note, I believe these types of t-shirts Joe wore during this tour -- more specifically, the various messages he wrote on them -- and the band's more laid-back approach was not only very representative of the state of the music industry but Def Leppard's attitude and response to the situation.

Change was undeniably in the air at this time, as the band's popularity was starting to wane, and peoples' music tastes were shifting to other genres like grunge. So Def Leppard made a conscious decision: make it all about the music, and no need for elaborate concert theatrics.

The band was confident the quality of their music would endure, and they knew their dedicated fan base would stick it out with them through turbulent times. They just had to ride it out. And to those who moved on, or thought the band was no longer current or commercially appealing, and that Def Leppard's music had become passé, well, the band's message back to those people was clear: *Do Me.*

To further the point for just a moment, another one of Joe's t-shirts on that tour had the word "Slut" spray-painted on it. Take that for what you will, as it can certainly be forthright, but the impression I got, even more so in retrospect, was the expendable position the band was increasingly finding itself in.

Radio stations that couldn't get enough of Def Leppard's music in previous years were losing interest and playing less of it, if at all, as they changed formats to accommodate the latest music flavor of the month. MTV was moving away from supporting the band's videos, too. Retail accounts and record stores were becoming less apt to promote the band on their limited shelf space. Case in point, it was convenient for them to "utilize" -- more specifically, monetize -- Def Leppard when the gettin' was good and to their benefit. But now, in the mid-'90s? Not so much, as the band was all of a sudden considered dispensable.

Is it a coincidence that *Slang* was the next studio album the band put out after this period? I think not.

So back to those t-shirt messages. On the surface, amusing and entertaining. But beneath the surface, a deeper, subliminal meaning resided that was open for interpretation.

At least that's my opinion.

Personal Story: Where Does Love Go When It Dies? Right Here!

Sometimes it's the quieter moments that resonate the loudest and leave a most wonderful memory.

One such moment which left me with that impression was during Def Leppard's *Slang* tour. It wasn't the concert itself, nor did it occur during a meet and greet or after-show get-together. Rather, it happened earlier in the day, when I had the unique opportunity to observe something I never had the chance to up to that point.

This was during the time the band was touring outdoor venues, aka sheds, where the stage faced thousands of reserved amphitheater seats, usually with a large grassy area for general admission tickets in the back for additional concertgoers to sit down and lay on to enjoy the show.

On this specific tour date, tasks such as setting up the meet and greet area for later that day -- where invited radio station and retail reps, contest winners, and other last-minute additions would congregate to have their opportunity to meet Def Leppard (or whichever band members would be participating in that day's promotional event) -- were completed early. (This was *way* before meet and greets were simply offered for purchase.)

With all the day's preparations ready to go ahead of schedule, I decided to take advantage of the free time to enjoy a walk around the entire outdoor venue, and take in what I always considered a very unique ambiance: the calm before the storm.

It was such a tranquil atmosphere, sometimes eerily quiet, knowing the sounds of thunderous cheers, screams and applause would be reverberating throughout the premises just hours later.

Walking the grounds, I eventually made my way to the venue's completely empty seating area, row upon row of seemingly endless seats that were unoccupied.

As timing would have it, soundcheck was happening, and all of Def Leppard's members were on the stage, going through their preparations.

From a fan's perspective, it was remarkable to witness: there was no parading around the stage and playing to a crowd (figuratively and literally); no awe-inspiring light show occurring in lockstep with the band's stage movements; typical concert attire gave way to (even) more casual, everyday outfits, and so on. None of the things one would expect when normally seeing Def Leppard on a stage.

It was a genuine peek at the guys being themselves and doing their thing -- chatting, exchanging ideas, as they focused on their work and went about their stage show preparations; testing out how their instruments were sounding at the venue, performing a portion of a song here and there, and so on.

I know this isn't all that surprising, as fans would expect any band to go through the motions of soundcheck, but that doesn't negate the fact that it isn't something a fan would typically witness.

Consequently, I felt it was too good of a rare glimpse to pass up!

So I moseyed over to one of the venue's empty seats, around 20 or so rows back, and sat down to soak up the special moment.

There are so many great Def Leppard concert memories and experiences I enjoyed back then, but this was one of the *really* special ones.

Even while feeling I shouldn't have been there so the guys could warm up without any audience whatsoever, I decided I would linger for a little bit, at least long enough to hear a good portion of a song, and if at any moment one of the band members told me to leave, so be it!

Fortunately, that didn't happen.

Within a couple of minutes after sitting down and watching the band go through their prep, with individual members playing piecemeal parts of songs to test out on the venue's acoustics, the warm-up session advanced to the band actually performing a song collectively: "Where Does Love Go When It Dies," a personal favorite from the band's *Slang* album and a setlist rarity, especially on subsequent tours.

The performance echoed around the empty venue, which made the moment feel all the more riveting and impactful.

Being the mid-90s, holding up a smartphone to capture the performance, or having pictures or video taken to immediately post on social media with a few clicks of a button, wasn't an option, which only contributes to what made this moment so genuine and special, and for that matter, less invasive from the band's point of view.

It simply involved me just taking it all in and enjoying the moment, as surreal as it was.

I've been asked over the years if I have a favorite Def Leppard concert. There certainly are many that are special for plenty of unique reasons, but having the band perform, of all things, rarely-played gem "Where Does Love Go When It Dies" in a venue with an audience of practically one, as if the concert was being put on just for you, well, that's unforgettable.

Single Spotlight: "Women"

In the beginning...

Def Leppard's *Hysteria* album required a powerhouse track to catapult, not to mention reintroduce, the band back into the public eye, particularly after such a prolonged hiatus since the heyday of *Pyromania*.

The album undoubtedly featured a plethora of songs that were capable of taking on the critical role of lead single to rekindle Def Leppard's star, which undeniably had lost some of its luster through no fault of the band.

It was only a matter of making a choice that also kept the album's long-term promotional plan in mind. "Pour Some Sugar On Me"? It would make more sense for *Hysteria*'s single strategy to approach its apex before releasing a song like that. "Love Bites"? Best to hold off and not release the album's premier power ballad prematurely. Title track "Hysteria"? While arguably the album's best song, having a mid-tempo track launch an album being positioned as the "rock version of Michael Jackson's *Thriller*" could have been counterproductive.

There were still numerous song options that could have fit right in with radio station playlists in 1987 -- from "Animal" to "Armageddon It" to even "Excitable," with its "State of Shock"-like groove. ("State of Shock," a song by The Jacksons and featuring Mick Jagger, was a chart success as a Top 5 hit years prior.)

With all that in mind, the song chosen as *Hysteria*'s vital first single, to conquer U.S. radio stations and reengage long lost Def Leppard fans, would be..."Women." A unique, solid song, but one better suited as a deep cut, especially when compared to the album's other radio-friendly offerings.

But There Was Something Missing, Something (A Single Opportunity) Lost

As the story goes, Def Leppard's management at the time believed "Women" was the pick of the litter as far as lead singles go, whereas the band preferred "Animal" (which was *Hysteria*'s first official single in the U.K.).

To be fair, "Women" in and of itself is a terrific track, perfectly placed in the lead-off spot on *Hysteria*'s tracklisting. The moment its iconic guitar introduction begins, a mood is set, immediately reinforced by a pulsating rhythm, prominent bass line, and sonically bombastic drums. Speaking of which, if memory serves, I recall Rick Allen telling an interviewer back in the late-'80s that one of his electronic drum kit's pre-programmed sounds resembled, well, to put it nicely, the end result of an elephant's bowel movement -- specifically, what it would probably sound like when something of that elephantine size hits the pavement. (That's an analogy I don't think I'll ever forget, especially whenever hearing those smashing -- splatting? -- drum effects during "Women.")

Digestive comparisons aside, "Women" was -- and still is -- an essential track on the *Hysteria* album, but that doesn't necessarily mean it ever qualified as a *mainstream* single. Moreover, nearly one minute was removed from the song for its diluted "radio edit" release, further conveying a single choice that equated to forcing a square peg into a round hole.

Upon its release, *some* rock radio stations supported

"Women." As for Top 40 (i.e., mainstream) radio stations, which were the primary target -- not so much. Not by a mile.

Def Leppard -- a band whose *Pyromania* album relentlessly hovered near the top of the album chart, with songs that were practically impossible to avoid hearing on radio stations across the country -- had finally returned with brand new music, and all "Women" could muster in its debut week on *Billboard*'s Hot 100 singles chart was #94. A weak start, to say the least.

Hopes of chart momentum picking up in its second week were quickly dashed when "Women" only moved up to #86. By the third week of its single run, it reached its *peak* chart position: #80. It would fall back down the charts in the two weeks that followed and then disappear altogether.

The chart life for *Hysteria*'s first U.S. single, the one whose main objective was to loudly and proudly proclaim "We're back!" to Def Leppard fans and American audiences far and wide, lasted on the charts for only 5 measly weeks.

The track did crack the Top 10 on *Billboard*'s less significant Mainstream Rock chart, but the band needed something more -- much more -- to reestablish themselves with fans and potential music consumers. "Women" most certainly didn't accomplish this goal, which isn't all that surprising for another reason -- reviewing what songs were ruling the Hot 100 chart at the time.

The week "Women" peaked, the #1 song on the Hot 100 chart was "La Bamba" by Los Lobos, while #2 was "I Just Can't Stop Loving You" by Michael Jackson (dueting with Siedah Garrett). Rounding out the Top 5: "Who's That Girl" by Madonna; "Only In My Dreams" by Debbie Gibson; "Didn't We Almost Have It All" by Whitney Houston.

A track like "Women" fits right in with those songs, right? Maybe not.

But there was encouraging data elsewhere on the chart.

There was a track that entered the Top 10 at #8 the same week "Women" peaked: Whitesnake's "Here I Go Again," which went on to reach the #1 position before quickly dropping off.

The same week "Here I Go Again" topped the chart, another notable track held the #3 slot (where it also peaked): Europe's ballad "Carrie."

These were signs of things to come. Music tastes were expanding, if not shifting. Melodic, radio-friendly rock songs and power ballads were leveling the playing field on the charts, presenting a more accommodative music environment for a band like Def Leppard to pounce on. So even though "Women" didn't work out, at some point, *Hysteria*'s arsenal of other, stronger single candidates would, in all likelihood, find better success.

Ironically, the B-side for the "Women" single was the rawer, yet more melodic, rock track "Tear It Down." Had that song been on the *Hysteria* album and released as the lead-off single, it's plausible that it would have outperformed "Women." Of course, we'll never know, but it's fun to sometimes contemplate these types of hypotheticals.

"Women" Lives On

Regardless of its shortfall on the charts, "Women" was still a stalwart on Def Leppard's *Hysteria* tour setlist, even making it onto some setlists for future tours. It's no doubt a crowd-pleaser when performed live -- most notably during Def Leppard's *Viva Hysteria!* Las Vegas residency, when it kicked off the band's main show. (Phil Collen would appear out of the darkness on a raised platform, alone with guitar in hand, and begin to play the song's distinctive opening notes. Synchronized fists pumping in the air and "*Women!*" chorus chants from the audience would soon follow.)

"Women" not being a radio hit, yet appearing on multiple Def Leppard tours since *Hysteria*, makes its repeated setlist inclusion all the more special and a rarity; after all, the track wasn't included on the band's first greatest hits release, *Vault*. And though it was part of the *Rock of Ages: The Definitive Collection* release, it wasn't part of any of the configurations for *The Story So Far* greatest hits release.

Final Thoughts

Hysteria had seven U.S. singles, an amazing feat for an album of its type, but, frankly, it's a stretch to refer to "Women" as one of the album's "hit" singles, which it commonly is.

"Seven hit singles!" works splendidly from a marketing perspective, but that requires "Women" to have been part of that equation, and unless simply scratching *Billboard*'s Hot 100 singles chart qualifies, it doesn't pass the "hit single" test. Arguably, reaching the Top 10 on the singles chart could define a song as a bona fide "hit," but so could merely making it into the Top 40. Regardless, peaking at the #80 position and calling it a "hit" could more than likely be considered an overstatement.

Determining whether "Women" legitimately qualifies as a hit single may be moot, if not futile, decades after its release, but pondering whether *Hysteria* could truly have had seven or even eight hit singles -- courtesy of "Excitable" and "Love And Affection" -- instead of "Women" expending one of those precious slots is an entertaining thought.

Most importantly, the underperformance of "Women" could have derailed the *Hysteria* release and the album's promotional strategy out of the box, but it didn't. Slow start aside, the album was fortunate to have strong(er) offerings waiting to turn the tide. It was only a matter of time, especially with an increasingly amicable radio landscape, that Def Leppard would unleash an "Animal" of a single and regain some airplay momentum.

Just because "Women" lacks a wondrous success story like

many of its single counterparts doesn't diminish the song's quality. It remains a beloved track and a highlight when performed live. It's also an essential component of the *Hysteria* album's listening experience. And, chart performance be damned, that's a whole lotta something you can't sacrifice.

Single Spotlight: "Hysteria"

Def Leppard's song "Hysteria" may very well be a magical mysteria, especially in how it packs a wallop as powerful as any of the *Hysteria* album's most bombastic tracks.

It's not a power ballad. It would be a bit of a stretch to even classify it as a ballad per se, at least a typical one. Referring to "Hysteria" as a mid-tempo pop-rock song might be more appropriate.

The elusiveness to label "Hysteria" only adds to its mystique. And while it's delicate and subtle in its approach, it grasps listeners and places them under its mighty spell right from the outset.

The song's positioning on the *Hysteria* album's tracklisting is quite fitting, too. Once you get beyond the opening track "Women," the first half of the album ("Side 1") overflows with a slew of massive, radio-friendly hit singles. Meanwhile, the second half ("Side 2") contains the album's "deeper" cuts. And in the middle of that assortment, "Hysteria" makes its appearance. It's a bit unexpected and almost sneaks up on a listener, yet it still doesn't seem out of place as it's sandwiched between "Run Riot" and "Excitable." It assuredly holds its own, standing out from the "Side 2" pack.

It's also worth mentioning that Def Leppard did a splendid job visually capturing the essence of the song with its classy, memorable music video. From its dancehall setting to its dimly lit mood lighting, not to mention the band's choice of wardrobe, the video embodies and reinforces the elegance of the track. (Frankly, there have been times when a Def Leppard music video has *detracted* from a song, "Tonight" being one of them. "Hysteria" is definitely *not* one of those instances.)

When You Get That Feelin', Better Start Recording It!

"Hysteria" is a prime example of Def Leppard's method of song creation synchronicity.

As you may have already read elsewhere in this book, the band is known to sometimes piece together *completely different* ideas brought forward by band members, which then results in the creation of an entirely new song.

Phil Collen explained how the song "Hysteria" came about to *Goldmine Magazine*:

> "We pieced together that song. I remember we were sitting in Dublin, and Rick Savage goes, "Oh, I've got this riff." He played it, and I literally just sung the first verse. It was the first thing that came out of my head and I was like, "Write this down; record it." We did the next bit. It literally happened so quickly that we had half of the song. We took it to Steve, Mutt and Joe, and it turned out to be something else."

Between all its nuances, "Hysteria" magnificently showcases each band member's talents right alongside its hard-to-resist melodies and harmonies: Joe Elliott's rich, emotive vocals; the finely textured guitars layered on by Steve Clark and Phil Collen; Rick Savage's smooth and steady bass line; the hypnotic groove of Rick Allen's drumming.

Producer Robert John "Mutt" Lange and engineer Mike Shipley (who handled the mixing) also deserve major accolades for making "Hysteria" a reality. Without their creative input and technical wizardry, the song would not have been the gem it turned out to be.

Chart Performance

"Hysteria" was the third single off of the *Hysteria* album in the U.S. (following up "Women" and "Animal"), and continued the album's streak of every single release outperforming its predecessor on the charts. "Hysteria" became the album's first Top 10 single, peaking at #10. (The upward chart streak on *Billboard*'s Hot 100 singles chart would continue, as "Pour Some Sugar On Me" followed it up, reaching #2; "Love Bites" then came next, reaching #1.)

Might the single chart performance of "Hysteria" have been even better if it were released *after* a juggernaut like "Pour Some Sugar on Me," which resulted in *Hysteria*'s album sales, radio support, and overall awareness to skyrocket? Potentially.

In the end, it doesn't matter, as a #1 single does not always a great song make, and "Hysteria" soared regardless.

Still Hysterical After All These Years

"Hysteria" is a mainstay on Def Leppard's tour setlist; it would be sacrilegious to *not* include it. (The same can be said about numerous other songs in the band's catalog, which is a whole other discussion.)

The track is still well-received and as popular as ever with concertgoers. The band's live performance is more straightforward these days, as opposed to the *Hysteria* tour, when they teased audiences with an extended, ambiguous introduction, leaving them guessing for a brief period (which also allowed Joe Elliott to take a quick break). It wouldn't be until the song's classic melody kicked in that its identity would finally be revealed, to the delight of those in attendance.

"Hysteria" (Take 2)

Before making their catalog available digitally, and due to what seemed like a never-ending royalty dispute over digital sales with their record company, Def Leppard re-recorded (nearly) identical versions of several tracks and released them themselves.

It's no surprise one of the songs the band chose to re-record in 2013 was "Hysteria." While the term "imitated but never duplicated" could apply, Def Leppard's effort was respectable, despite the newer version's inability to completely (and impossibly) replicate the inimitable magic of the original.

Fortunately, it's now a moot point, as the band's entire catalog was finally released digitally in 2018, allowing a whole new generation to discover and enjoy the songs as they were originally intended.

Oh, Can You Feel It? Fans Still Do!

"Hysteria" isn't the band's loudest or most anthemic track, yet it's Def Leppard at their *Hysteria*-era best.

Certain Def Leppard songs can transport you to a different time and place the very moment you hear their opening chords; "Hysteria" unfailingly achieves this remarkable feat.

As for the song's true meaning and ultimate message, Phil Collen explained it to Songfacts:

> "The song really is about finding spiritual enlightenment. Not many people know that because it sounds like just getting hysterical, but it's actually about that. It's about finding this deeper thing, whether you believe it

or not."

Oh, can you feel it? Do you believe it? Def Leppard fans certainly still do.

Single Spotlight: "Pour Some Sugar On Me"

Def Leppard's "Pour Some Sugar On Me" single was released in the U.S. in April 1988. (The U.K. release occurred months earlier, in September 1987.)

The iconic song was the fourth U.S. single off of the band's *Hysteria* album.

"Pour Some Sugar On Me" is also included on the band's *Vault*, *Rock of Ages: The Definitive Collection*, and *The Story So Far* releases. In other words, *all* of Def Leppard's greatest hits albums.

The Music Video (Take Two)

The "Pour Some Sugar On Me" music video played a vital role in the song's epic success, but it required two attempts to get it right.

The original version ("the U.K. version") featured the band performing the song while confined to a house falling apart around them. It was light-hearted and even brought to mind the band's memorable "Me & My Wine" music video, perhaps as its pseudo-sequel: that same rowdy bunch of guys *still* refuse to move out, even now as their building is being demolished!

But was this music video and its claustrophobic setting effective in capturing the magnitude of a song like "Pour Some Sugar On Me"? No.

Enter the "live in concert" music video version.

The second version ("the U.S. version") undoubtedly improved on the "building demolition" video premise, just as the band had hoped.

For starters, it featured a much more powerful opening: the impactful *"Love is like a bomb, bomb, bomb..."* extended intro instead of the tame-by-comparison *"Step inside, walk this way, you and me, babe. Hey! Hey!"* from the song's album version.

The concert music video version also added a whole new element of pulse-quickening energy to the song, effectively capturing the anticipation and excitement of Def Leppard's *Hysteria* in-the-round show: starting with frenetic shots of the tour's massive lighting rigs and a draped-off stage (not to mention Rick Savage fooling around for the camera, to the amusement of viewers).

Subtle enhancements were also made to the music video's audio track, which made a *huge* difference: inserting the sound effect of an ever-present concert audience buzzing throughout the song's performance; sweetening the song's shout-out-loud chorus with a minor echo to further get across the atmospherics of a jam-packed arena.

Collectively, these improvements worked splendidly in encapsulating a Def Leppard concert experience.

The band took care of the rest, as director Wayne Isham expertly showcased their rousing performance throughout -- from the theatrics of Phil Collen and Steve Clark playing the song's monster riffs as only they can, to Rick Allen living up to his "Thunder God" persona, to Joe Elliott -- in his iconic *Hysteria* tour outfit comprised of shredded blue jeans and a cut-up "Women of Doom" shirt -- playing to the crowd.

The band knew they captured lightning in a bottle with this

video version, as did their record company; after sending out promotional copies of the music video to networks like MTV for airplay consideration, it was only a matter of time.

I Want My MTV...To Play 'Sugar'!

"Pour Some Sugar On Me" ended up earning the top video spot on MTV's show "Dial MTV" for several months in a row, and also landed atop (or near the top, depending on when the network would update its rankings) of MTV's "Greatest Music Videos of All-Time" list.

Back in the late '80s, Joe Elliott once humbly, yet proudly, commented about the U.S. version of the "Pour Some Sugar On Me" video in an MTV interview, remarking *"It's good, isn't it?"*

"Good" doesn't describe it. "Momentous" would have been a better term, as the video was a major factor in not only raising the song's awareness but also elevating Def Leppard's popularity to all-new heights.

Pour Some Sugar On Me? What A Great Idea!

As documented numerous times over the years, "Pour Some Sugar On Me" originated from Joe Elliott simply messing around on an acoustic guitar during a break in the recording studio while wrapping up the *Hysteria* album.

Fortunately, Joe's idea caught the ear of producer Mutt Lange, who immediately felt a gem of a song could be constructed from it.

The rest is history.

Love Is Like A...What?

"Pour Some Sugar On Me" successfully combines metaphors

and sexual innuendos with vague, nonsensical lyrics that sound great phonetically, but don't necessarily have any meaning.

For instance, the origin of the song's unforgettable opening line *"Love is like a bomb."* Joe Elliott explained how it came about on the *Hysteria* episode of the "Classic Albums" documentary series:

> *"Myself and Mutt Lange had dictaphones and we actually just went to opposite ends of the control room while it was playing and just made noises over the backing track and swapped machines and started translating what we thought the words were, and the first line on Mutt's tapes, to me, sounded like 'Love is like a bomb'...and that set the whole tone for the lyric."*

That's not to say Joe's music influences didn't also make their way into the song -- after all, "Sugar Sugar" by The Archies (reportedly, the first record Joe ever bought) does include the line *"Pour a little sugar on me, baby..."*!

Topping The Charts Isn't Everything

"Love Bites" may officially be considered Def Leppard's "biggest" hit because it reached #1 on *Billboard*'s Hot 100 singles chart, but "Pour Some Sugar On Me" is arguably the track that had the greatest overall impact on the *Hysteria* album's success.

It was "Pour Some Sugar On Me" that caught everyone's attention: radio stations and MTV fell in love with it and supported it with what seemed like endless heavy rotation. As a result, record stores could barely keep *Hysteria* in stock, with *several million copies* being sold during the single's run.

That's how significant "Pour Some Sugar On Me" was.

The song provided Def Leppard with the opportunity to reclaim the mainstream pop culture spotlight, and not only revisit but surpass the immense success they enjoyed with *Pyromania*.

"Pour Some Sugar On Me" also perfectly positioned follow-up single "Love Bites" to reach an established mass audience, resulting in the band's first #1 hit in the U.S. and, subsequently, adding even more sales momentum to the *Hysteria* album and tour.

Unlike "Love Bites," though, "Pour Some Sugar On Me" peaked at #2 on *Billboard*'s singles chart. Regardless, between the two songs, it's practically impossible to imagine a Def Leppard concert without "Pour Some Sugar On Me" on the setlist.

Def Leppard Will Continue To Pour Some Sugar

"Pour Some Sugar On Me" was not only one of the biggest songs of the late-'80s, if not the decade, but it also remains one of the band's most important.

The song took on a life of its own, and, for better or worse, is the track many people will always associate with Def Leppard.

It's not surprising Joe Elliott was asked during a 2019 TV interview with *Good Morning America* -- decades after the song's release -- to literally pour some sugar into a mug for the interviewer's nostalgic amusement.

It's also no surprise that Joe filmed a humorous, surreal video in 2018 which went viral titled "Pouring Sugar with Joe Elliott" based around the song's title. The video captured him pouring sugar onto items and witnessing the magic that results! Fans ate it up, pun intended.

Final Thoughts

Def Leppard has performed "Pour Some Sugar On Me" in concert thousands of times. They know it's wanted and expected from the majority of live audiences, and that's why the song will always remain a staple in the band's setlist.

Several decades after its release, the song continues to stir up excitement among concertgoers. It's an event in and of itself to hear it performed live and sing along to, and will always be one of the most memorable high points of a Def Leppard show.

To this day, many fans still crave their 'Sugar' fix, and they always will -- in the name of love and Def Leppard!

Single Spotlight: "Love Bites"

Def Leppard's "Love Bites" single was released in the U.S. in August 1988. (The U.K. release occurred in July 1988.)

No surprise, the track is also included in every one of the band's greatest hits releases -- *Vault, Rock of Ages: The Definitive Collection,* and *The Story So Far.*

If You've Got A Hit Single In Your Sights, Watch Out

"Love Bites" epitomized Def Leppard's monstrous *Hysteria* album success in the late '80s. Let us count just some of the ways.

Hysteria's preceding single, "Pour Some Sugar On Me," was a phenomenon, ruling radio airwaves over the summer of '88, and propelling the band's popularity -- and, importantly, consumer interest in the album -- to stratospheric heights. Yet 'Sugar' did *not* reach #1 on *Billboard*'s Hot 100 singles chart, peaking at #2. Being unable to classify the song as an official "chart-topper," though, doesn't at all diminish what a career shape-shifter it was for Def Leppard.

Given that, "Love Bites" had the unenviable task of being the follow-up single to "Pour Some Sugar On Me," to keep *Hysteria*'s tremendous sales and tour momentum going. Not only did "Love Bites" reach the #2 chart slot achieved by 'Sugar,' it surpassed it, rewarding Def Leppard with yet another crowning achievement: the band's first-ever #1 single -- a feat, unfairly or not, never accomplished by juggernaut "Pour Some Sugar On Me."

Moreover, it's also worth noting that the single run for "Love Bites" happened more than *one year* after the *Hysteria* album was released. Talk about sustainability: "Love Bites" was the album's *fifth* U.S. single and its top performer, remaining on the singles chart for a whopping 23 weeks ('Sugar' charted for 24 weeks), further reaffirming the depth and strength of the iconic album's offerings.

"Love Bites" was another reminder of how far Def Leppard had come, a band whose peak popularity during the *Pyromania* era would have seemed all but impossible to repeat. Yet they did: *Pyromania* sold a massive amount of records; *Hysteria* sold more. *Pyromania*'s success included a huge tour in support of it; *Hysteria*'s tour was bigger. *Pyromania*'s singles, while iconic, didn't reach the Top 10 on the U.S. charts; *Hysteria*'s tracks made it into the Top 10 on multiple occasions, and with "Love Bites" reaching the #1 spot, it solidified its place on Def Leppard's mantel of song accomplishments.

Let's take an even deeper dive into Def Leppard's #1 power ballad.

Who Do You Think Of, Does He Look Like...Mutt

It is not an embellishment to proclaim that "Love Bites" would not have happened without the involvement of *Hysteria*'s producer, Robert John "Mutt" Lange.

Def Leppard songs like "Pour Some Sugar On Me" and "Hysteria" originated with a band member's idea, be it a power chord or melody. As for "Love Bites," it wasn't an instance of Joe Elliott fooling around on an acoustic guitar, which resulted in "Pour Some Sugar On Me," or Rick Savage and Phil Collen piecing together separate song portions to create what would become "Hysteria."

"Love Bites" originated with Mutt Lange. Not only that, the original version Mutt had written was more in the vein of a country song, before being Leppard-ized. Early on, additional lyrics were also recorded, courtesy of Mutt, for the song's pre-chorus, to counter and balance out lines like *"I don't want to touch you too much baby,"* but they ended up being scrapped for the track's final version. (Check out the release *Classic Albums: Hysteria*, which is available on DVD and digitally, to hear some of those original lines performed by Mutt Lange.)

Mutt Lange's fingerprints are all over "Love Bites," most notably during the song's chorus, where his trademark backing vocals are prominently featured. Nevertheless, "Love Bites" succeeds at ultimately being a classic Def Leppard track through and through.

A Golden Leppard Age

1988 was a golden age -- if not, *the* golden age -- for Def Leppard's brand of music. Case in point: "Hysteria," "Pour Some Sugar On Me," "Love Bites," and "Armageddon It" were all released as U.S. singles during that same year.

Arguably, the band could do no wrong and was mostly competing against itself in terms of chart performance, as all of those 1988 singles reached the Top 10, with the majority of them making it into the Top 3.

It was a most welcoming radio environment, as other top chart performers around that time included the likes of Poison ("Every Rose Has Its Thorn"), Guns N' Roses ("Sweet Child O' Mine"), and Bon Jovi ("Bad Medicine").

There was no wave of alternative music or grunge movements to battle against. No substantial rise in flannel shirt sales just yet either; instead, Def Leppard fans proudly wore their "Women of Doom" t-shirts in classrooms throughout the country, some even going so far as to wear them to class with razor-blade-shredded denim jeans (guilty as charged), which mixed in well with the attire of fellow classmates, who'd be wearing their own favorite band on a t-shirt: Gun N' Roses, Van Halen, Bon Jovi, Whitesnake, Poison, and so on. It was a communal-like experience, where you were making a fashion statement while proudly sharing who your band of choice was with others.

Surely, this is a protracted example, but there is a broader point to get across: *That* is what 1988 was like for that type of music -- the halcyon days of its pop-culture influence and dominance at radio stations and record stores, and something that would never be repeated.

For those of you that lived through this period yourself, I have no doubt you can relate and likely have your own stories to tell.

The Music Video

The "Love Bites" music video was dimly lit and moody, which was not only fitting for the song but also 1988. Frankly, at this point in *Hysteria*'s reign, most fans simply wanted more Def Leppard -- more singles, more music videos, more tour dates, etc. Most were content with *anything* the band would put out. (Fans who purchased Def Leppard's *Historia* release on VHS early on -- you know who you are -- were pleasantly surprised with the "Love Bites" music video before it had even "world premiered" on MTV. It was included soon after *Historia*'s main program ended, a pseudo-Easter egg before there were DVD Easter eggs, or DVDs, for that matter.)

Final Thoughts

Decades after its release, "Love Bites" is still performed on tour, with a live version that showcases a notably more melodic pre-chorus, due in no small part to Vivian Campbell's backing vocal contributions.

"Love Bites" was a massive hit all its own, which can sometimes work against it, as there are some fans who wouldn't mind *not* hearing the song performed in concert again, or at least for a very long time. (The same can be said about some of Def Leppard's other mega-hits.) But how could Def Leppard *not* have "Love Bites" be part of their setlist? Not only is the song their first and only #1 hit, but it also provides the band (and those in attendance) with a tactical cool-down concert moment, most likely right before the momentum picks right up again with an arsenal of Def Leppard hits for the show's crescendo.

"Love Bites" had a critical mission, which it accomplished handily: keep the *Hysteria* album's momentum going by garnering a great deal of radio airplay (Check!); reach a wide, mainstream audience and convert new listeners into purchasing the single and album (Check! Check!); drive fans, new and old, toward (i.e. buy tickets for) the band's epic *Hysteria* tour. (Check!)

The song did such a splendid job during its single run that the *Hysteria* album reached #1 on *Billboard*'s album chart *again*, then comfortably resided within the Top 3 slots for what seemed like eons.

Love lives, love dies, but the fact that "Love Bites" remains very much alive and a fan favorite decades after its release, is definitely no surprise.

Single Spotlight (And A Personal One At That!): "Rocket"

There are plenty of songs in Def Leppard's catalog that epitomize what the band is all about: "Photograph," with its gargantuan power chords and masterful melodies; the anthemic, bombastic "Pour Some Sugar On Me"; the escapism and tongue-in-cheek humor of "Let's Get Rocked," among many others.

But one song truly embodies Def Leppard's foundation and the band's roots: "Rocket."

Let's travel through the center of the dark for this in-depth look back at the song.

The Year Was 1989

There are subtleties, at least in some respects, within the lyrics for "Rocket."

I clearly recall a moment in high school, when "Rocket," which was receiving heavy rotation on radio stations and MTV at the time, became the topic of discussion with a couple of my classmates. (Yes, I was a passionate Def Leppard fan even back then.)

One of them asked me, "What's that line they sing in 'Rocket'? Satellite of...love?" (For the record, the fellow students

I was talking to were Def Leppard fans as well, but to a much lesser extent; they were more in the Guns N' Roses camp of late '80s rock bands, which then morphed into becoming grunge music fans when that era emerged a few years later.)

After confirming that "Satellite of Love" was indeed the song lyric, they laughed, one of them then proclaiming "That's so dumb," not realizing the historical reference to Lou Reed's classic song.

Putting this oh-so profound hallway chat aside, it does shine a light on the perceptions *and* misperceptions of Def Leppard's music. Whether considered "heavy metal" early on in the band's career or quickly being dismissed as a "hair band" after grunge overtook radio airwaves in the '90s, it's fairly easy to overlook Def Leppard's origins and musical influences in the whole labeling process.

There are some who are "casual" Def Leppard fans whose favorite tracks don't extend much beyond, say, "Photograph," "Love Bites," or "Pour Some Sugar On Me," which is fine, more power to them. But there is absolutely a lot more beneath the surface to discover, and to appreciate the artists Def Leppard subtly (and not so subtly) honors in its music.

For some, "Jack Flash" and "Rocket Man" may come across as silly lyrics at first, and perhaps, for the uninitiated, even "Sergeant Pepper and the band." Just like a seemingly nonsensical, foolish -- or in high school speak, "dumb" -- line like "Satellite of Love." But fans of The Rolling Stones, Elton John, The Beatles, and Lou Reed would most likely have a different interpretation and appreciation.

"Rocket" has a unique lyrical style, with its verses structured in such a way that they're sung as if they're being read off of a checklist, kind of like a who's-who and a what's-what. (Billy Joel's classic song "We Didn't Start The Fire" resembled the same checklist-like lyric structure, to an even greater degree, when it hit radio airwaves a little over two years after the *Hysteria* album's release.)

Never-Ending *Hysteria*

"Rocket" was *Hysteria*'s final single release. An edited version was specially created for mainstream radio stations (and used for the music video), which diminished the song's wallop somewhat, leaving its original six-plus minute version for AOR stations to lay claim to.

The song would go on to peak at #12 on *Billboard*'s Hot 100 singles chart, yet another great example exemplifying the depth of *Hysteria*. Even as its seventh single, and reaching the Top 15, there were arguably *still* other song offerings from the album that could've taken the seventh single slot, or followed up "Rocket" as singles of their own.

(Vinyl promo copy of the "Rocket" single sent to radio stations included a sticker that made light of the number of single releases from Hysteria.)

The Music Video

The "Rocket" music video, with its frenetic cuts showcasing newsreels and tributes to music icons throughout, effectively counterbalanced that footage with the band's performance in a warehouse. (More on that in a moment.)

On its surface, the video had a celebratory look and a big-budget feel. To nitpick, though, the editing of the band's performance could have been a wee bit tighter: it always irked me that the footage used of Joe Elliott singing to the camera at the video's 2:22 mark is the *same exact clip* that's used again later in the video, at about the 3:26 mark. I digress.

Upon deeper reflection, the "Rocket" music video appropriately bookends not only Def Leppard's success with the *Hysteria* album but as a band. The warehouse the video is filmed in is the same warehouse the band filmed their "Women" music video. Mull that over for a moment: During the "Women" video shoot, Def Leppard was a band with an uncertain future, millions of dollars in debt, and facing the nearly impossible task of repeating the sales success of *Pyromania*.

By the time "Rocket" was released, *Hysteria*'s sales not only matched *Pyromania*'s but far exceeded them. The uncertainties and concerns from the "Women" days were gone, and a much more confident and reassured Def Leppard had become one of the biggest bands in the world. It seemed appropriate that "Rocket" and its video spotlighted some of the band's influences who helped get them there, as they reached this pinnacle.

In hindsight, the "Rocket" music video is both nostalgic and melancholic for several reasons: these were the glory days of Def Leppard and *Hysteria*, something that inevitably would come to an end. Not only that, while the music video closes the chapter on *Hysteria*'s incredible journey, it also brings to light a more somber end-of-an-era realization: this would be the final Def Leppard music video that Steve Clark would appear in. A lot would change for the band after this point.

Still Traveling Through The Center Of The Dark

Def Leppard still performs "Rocket" in concert, and rightfully so: its iconic opening, larger-than-life drums, and sing-along chorus are just some of the reasons why.

The band has even utilized the track as their concert opener on tour, which, frankly, has its pros and cons. While "Rocket" works wonderfully when it's used as a lead-in to the band's setlist crescendo of massive hit songs, it comes across a bit anti-climactic as an opening number. The drums that launch the song certainly get the audience's adrenaline flowing, but having the band simply stand on stage staring out at the crowd for what seems like an extended period of time, at least until the song's instrument cues begin ("Guitar! Drums!"), is less conducive and not nearly as effective as other opening numbers the band has used.

To use a baseball analogy, "Rocket" is better suited batting further down the lineup (i.e., setlist) instead of being the lead-off hitter.

A more recent example where the song was effectively placed within Def Leppard's setlist was during the band's Planet Hollywood "Sin City" residency. During the show's final portion, "Rocket" kicked things into high gear as monster tracks "Let's Get Rocked," "Hysteria," "Love Bites," "Armageddon It," and "Pour Some Sugar On Me" followed it, before going to the encore.

For anyone who attended the "Sin City" residency on August 20, 2019, or may have seen video from the show on YouTube, there's a moment during the band's performance of "Rocket" when Joe sings the classic line I mentioned earlier -- *Jack Flash, Rocket Man, Sergeant Pepper and the band* -- to a person in the audience. He then follows it up by giving that particular audience member a high-five.

That person was me.

How fitting this happened during "Rocket," the same exact song this high school kid was defending to classmates about

30 years earlier.

Funny how things work out sometimes.

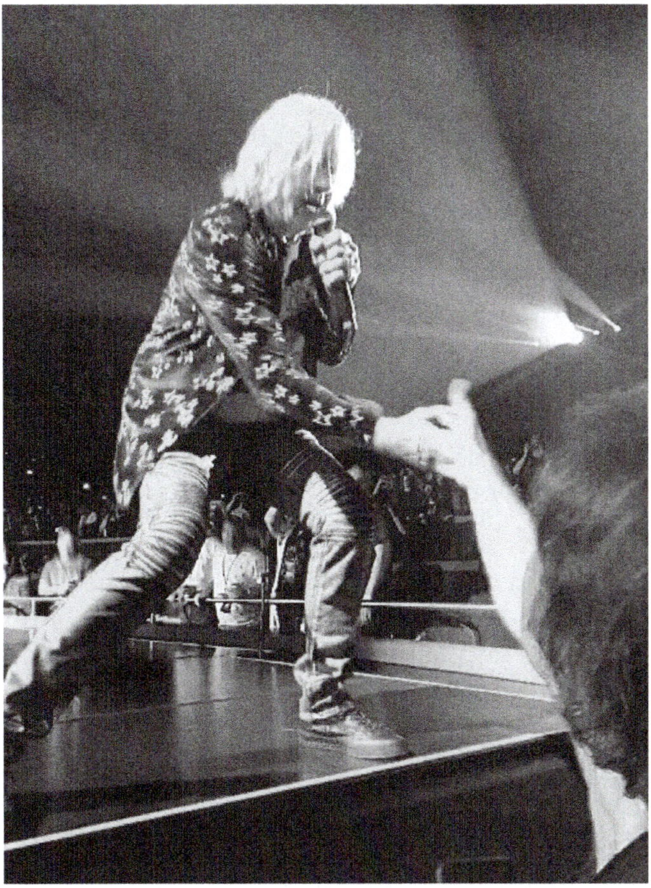

Single Spotlight: "Let's Get Rocked"

Def Leppard's "Let's Get Rocked" was unleashed onto radio stations in April 1992, and was the first single off of the band's eagerly awaited *Adrenalize* album.

"Let's Get Rocked" is also included in all of the band's greatest hits compilations: *Vault*, *Rock of Ages: The Definitive Collection*, and *The Story So Far*.

Do You Wanna? Do You Wanna?!

From the moment Joe Elliott asks the rhetorical question *"Do you wanna get rocked?"*, Def Leppard fans know they're in store for nearly five minutes of anthemic rock music loaded to the gills with the band's signature trademarks: a polished production, a wall of sound featuring thunderous drums, booming guitars, unmistakable power chords and massive hooks, all which lead into an infectious, shout-out-loud chorus.

Undoubtedly, "Let's Get Rocked" and its carefree take on life was also cathartic for the band (and its fans) back in 1992, still grieving from the tragic death of guitarist Steve Clark.

Instead of going down a darker path as some might have expected, the band took a decidedly lighthearted, feel-good approach with *Adrenalize* (with the exception of "White Lightning"), attempting to recapture the sonic escapism of *Hysteria*. "Let's Get Rocked" is a prime example.

The song's intended silliness didn't connect with everyone, though. Over the years, Joe Elliott has spoken out about how the song's tongue-in-cheek lyrics and humor went over the head of many music critics who were quick to dismiss "Let's Get Rocked," not giving it a fair chance.

Joe addressed the topic with *Kaos 2000*:

> "I have a line in the song, 'I suppose a rock's out of the question.' They [music critics] missed the point that it's supposed to be funny... They just see this overproduced, big, massive sound. In fact, that was exactly what we were trying to achieve."

Not My Style, Man!

The Bart Simpson character from *The Simpsons* TV series was the inspiration for "Let's Get Rocked," with the song's opening verse setting the tone with the line *"I'm your average, ordinary everyday kid. Happy to do nothin'..."* (Decades later, Homer Simpson joined forces with *Family Guy*'s Peter Griffin in the *Family Guy* episode "The Simpsons Guy," which includes its own, um, special tribute to Def Leppard's music.)

The song's intentionally juvenile premise was further spotlighted in Def Leppard's nothing-but-a-good-time "Let's Get Rocked" music video, where audiences were introduced to an animated teenage character named Flynn. The band even included the Flynn character on the *Adrenalize* tour's backstage passes. Here's one from my personal collection:

Even though Flynn ended up being more of a flash in the '90s pan, never to be seen again, fans still remember the character and what it represented, aptly summed up in the song's lyric *"Let's get out and play, rock the night away..."*

I Suppose A Top 10 Hit Is Out Of The Question?

"Let's Get Rocked" was a major turning point in Def Leppard's career -- in more ways than one.

The song was written by Joe Elliott, Phil Collen, Rick Savage, and Mutt Lange -- the same writing team behind all of *Hysteria*'s songs, with one glaring exception: Steve Clark.

"Let's Get Rocked" kicked off a new, Steve Clark-less era for the band.

The single release also marked a change to what had been Def Leppard's steadfast chart performance: "Let's Get Rocked" landed on *Billboard*'s Hot 100 singles chart at #27 -- an exceptionally strong, unprecedented, first-week debut for the band. (The chart feat was due to several factors, including pent-up interest and demand from fans who had waited years for a new Def Leppard song, robust sales of the CD single and cassingle out of the box, and a considerable amount of initial radio support.)

But *long-lasting* chart momentum, something that became commonplace during the days of *Pyromania* and *Hysteria*, had changed noticeably.

Normally, a single *debuting* at #27 would likely have enough momentum to peak near the top -- if not, *the* top -- of the Hot 100 singles charts. Yet after its powerful debut, "Let's Get Rocked" went from #27 to...#27 in its second week of release, not moving up at all.

In the third week of its single run, it practically stalled again, moving up *only one slot* to #26, before climbing a few more spots in its fourth week, landing at #18.

It crept up only three more slots to #15 in its fifth week, which is where it would peak -- disappointing, and a bit shocking, that after such a strong debut, "Let's Get Rocked" only climbed a total of twelve slots, and couldn't even reach the U.S. Top 10.

It was becoming clear that Def Leppard's days of releasing a single with a prolonged chart life were numbered (no pun intended). The chart performance for "Let's Get Rocked" was a warning sign, one that should have prompted the *Adrenalize* single release strategy to be revisited and recalibrated.

Unfortunately, going with yet another tongue-in-cheek song -- "Make Love Like A Man" -- as the album's second single was a misstep; the track underperformed, peaking at #36 on *Billboard*'s Hot 100 after only four weeks on the chart, further dampening *Adrenalize*'s sales momentum.

With the ever-present grunge movement unmistakably changing music tastes, Def Leppard single releases meaningfully climbing up the mainstream charts going forward would be far and few between.

Let's Get Rocked Again And Again

No matter the chart performance, it's more than likely that "Let's Get Rocked" will continue to be included on future Def Leppard concert setlists, as it remains a crowd favorite.

By the way, did you ever notice the band usually replaces the song's lyric *"Walk the dog!"* with *"Shag the dog!"* when they perform it live?

Final Thoughts

Simply accepting "Let's Get Rocked" for what it is -- a fun, bombastic, catchy song, which showcases Def Leppard's technical wizardry in the process -- makes the listening experience all the more enjoyable.

It's not surprising that it remains one of the band's most popular songs; decades after its release, it's abundantly clear that many Def Leppard fans most certainly *still* wanna get rocked.

Single Spotlight: "Make Love Like A Man"

Def Leppard's "Make Love Like A Man" single was released in June 1992.

The track is also included on Def Leppard's *Vault* (vinyl edition) and *The Story So Far* greatest hits releases.

Lyrically Speaking

A Def Leppard song having tongue-in-cheek lyrics isn't anything new. Take a glance through the band's catalog and you'll quickly find a handful of examples.

Conversely, there are times when the band's songwriting is quite subtle in conveying a deeper message. "Make Love Like A Man," however, is certainly not one of those instances.

Very straightforward in its delivery and humor, for better or worse, "Make Love Like A Man" is a prime example of the lighthearted direction Def Leppard pursued for their *Adrenalize* album. (After all, the album's lead single, "Let's Get Rocked," was inspired by "The Simpsons" television show.)

Whereas *Hysteria* offered up songs like "Women" and "Pour Some Sugar On Me," Def Leppard took their adoration of the female persuasion to a bolder level lyrics-wise, with *Adrenalize* tracks like "Personal Property," "I Wanna Touch U" ("*Till we're stuck like glue!*"), and, of course, "Make Love Like A Man."

Some may consider the lyrics to "Make Love Like A Man" blunt and crass, but that's what they were intended to be. Co-writer Phil Collen, who brought the song's concept to the band stated the original "*make love like a man*" lyric was only used as humorous filler until a better line could be crafted during the recording stage.

Meanwhile, Joe Elliott and Mutt Lange found Phil's original lyrics amusing and preferred to keep them as-is. (This should come as no surprise, especially for Mutt Lange, who's had his share of unconventional songs. For example, soon after, Mutt co-wrote the Bryan Adams songs "(I Wanna Be) Your Underwear" and "The Only Thing That Looks Good on Me Is You.")

Mr. Fun And Captain Cool

There's no point in attempting to dissect and analyze the lyrics to "Make Love Like A Man." They are simplistic and unambiguous, though lines like "*I'm a man, that's what I am*" makes one wonder if the band could have come up with something at least a little wittier.

But that's neither here nor there.

"Make Love Like A Man" is a playful song, and it's been included in many Def Leppard tour setlists over the years, gaining a new level of energy when its sing-along chorus is performed live. (It also provides Joe Elliott the opportunity to showcase his vocal chops by stretching out the word "*Better-r-r-r-r-r-r...*" at the song's end, holding the note to the delight of concert audiences.)

The Music Video

The easy-going atmosphere showcased in the "Make Love

Like A Man" music video is further emphasized by the band's lighthearted, just-having-a-good-time performance. In addition, the video featured old, silent film footage throughout to further reinforce the song's "romantic" message.

Notably, "Make Love Like A Man" was also Vivian Campbell's very first music video appearance as a member of Def Leppard.

Single Release Strategy

In hindsight, releasing "Make Love Like A Man" as Adrenalize's second single was a strategic misstep.

It was rather apparent by the time *Adrenalize* was released that the days of Def Leppard singles ruling the charts or lingering on them for long periods (i.e., the days of *Hysteria*) were just about gone.

Nirvana's "Smells Like Teen Spirit" already had its pop culture moment, and their *Nevermind* album had ruled *Billboard*'s chart just months before *Adrenalize*'s release. Change in mainstream music tastes was in the air, to put it mildly. All the more reason that the single selection plan for *Adrenalize* was of the utmost importance.

Things began commendably with "Let's Get Rocked," the album's first single. Sure, it was silly in its own right, and some fans may have felt a bit of a disconnect when comparing the track to Def Leppard songs they so fondly remembered from *Hysteria* and *Pyromania*, but, for the most part, it did its job as a lead-off single.

"Let's Get Rocked" exploded onto *Billboard*'s Hot 100 singles chart: It debuted at #27 -- an unprecedented starting position for a Def Leppard single, though not entirely surprising given the band's long-awaited return, the single's strong early sales, and initial radio support from major, influential stations.

But the single quickly started to lose momentum, stalling in its second week and remaining in the #27 slot.

Normally, a song *debuting* at number #27 on *Billboard*'s Hot 100 would be a safe bet to continue rocketing up the chart, potentially right into the Top 10, with a chance of even topping it at some point.

That didn't happen.

"Let's Get Rocked" *peaked* at #15, an impressive accomplishment in and of itself, but when looking at the broader picture, it was a clear indication that the band's streak of chart success and longevity was starting to wane.

Not only did "Let's Get Rocked" -- arguably the most radio-friendly rock track on *Adrenalize* -- not even reach the Top 10, but it topped out *only 6 weeks* into its run before falling back down the chart.

To put things in perspective, "Pour Some Sugar On Me" took 14 weeks to peak; even "Armageddon It" (the *sixth* single off of *Hysteria*) climbed the singles chart for 10 weeks before running out of fuel.

The fact that "Let's Get Rocked" didn't have a prolonged climb up the chart, especially after such a powerful debut, was both surprising and concerning. Alas, the music industry was swiftly transforming, and not in Def Leppard's favor, so it was vital to maintain radio airplay momentum going forward.

Don't Make Love Like A Man

"Let's Get Rocked" having a drastically shorter chart life than previous Def Leppard singles was a warning sign.

It was already a safe assumption that *Adrenalize* wasn't going to have the same kind of chart endurance as *Hysteria*, so striking while the album's proverbial iron was still hot, courtesy of another effective single, was crucial. That being said, "Make Love Like A Man" should *not* have been chosen as the next single release.

"Let's Get Rocked" showcased the "sillier" lyrical side of Def Leppard; following it up with an over-the-top song whose lyrics were *even sillier* wasn't helpful.

What should have been the second single? "I Wanna Touch U" and "Heaven Is" were radio-friendly options, though not as potent as "Let's Get Rocked." (Even though "Heaven Is" was never released as a single in the U.S., it was released in the U.K. and reached the Top 15.)

Timing-wise, "Tear It Down" arguably would have been a wise choice as the second single.

It's unfortunate that *Adrenalize's* version of "Tear It Down" somewhat diluted the song's earlier raw and edgy sound (the original version was the B-side for *Hysteria*'s "Women" single). Nevertheless, releasing "Tear It Down" as a single would have effectively showcased Def Leppard as *still* rocking hard, reminding listeners of the vintage power chords and hooks they most revered from the band.

Moreover, not only would the song have satisfied old-school fans, but it would have been an appealing offering for listeners discovering (or rediscovering) Def Leppard on the radio. This leads to one final point: "Tear It Down" would have elated *rock* radio stations, who would have supported the track and, essentially, *Adrenalize*.

Obviously, this scenario didn't happen.

The "Make Love Like A Man" single peaked at #36 after only *four* short weeks of climbing *Billboard*'s Hot 100 singles chart, and quickly disappeared, taking the air out of *Adrenalize*'s sails (and sales, to be more precise) in the process.

This doesn't dismiss the fact that *Adrenalize* achieved enormous early sales success. Not long after its release, the album was certified triple platinum in the U.S. alone -- very impressive, but it's also where its sales certification remains to this day; it never increased after that initial sales phase. Hence, the importance of trying to maintain the album's early sales momentum.

A good parallel to "Make Love Like A Man" is the *Hysteria* track "Excitable," a fun, catchy, and rather straightforward song (lyrically and musically). With that in mind, "Excitable" was once considered to be the *eighth* single off of the *Hysteria* album. Ultimately, it wasn't, but it still makes for a solid album track.

"Make Love Like A Man" would have been just fine following that same path, remaining an album track.

Final Thoughts

While "Make Love Like A Man" still goes over well when Def Leppard performs it live, the song's days of regular setlist inclusion are likely over, as even Joe Elliott has gone on the record saying he prefers to not perform it live, referring to the lyrics as a "nod too stupid." (Ironically, the band's self-titled *Def Leppard* album includes the track "Man Enough," a song whose main lyric is "*Are you man enough to be my girl*," apparently proving that Leppards can never completely change their spots.)

Whether releasing "Make Love Like A Man" as a single was the wrong decision no longer matters. It's just nice to know that decades after its release -- misstep or not -- Def Leppard survived the significant challenges of the 1990s.

Time will tell whether the band further shies away from "Make Love Like A Man" on future tours, but it remains an integral part of the *Adrenalize* album, and a song many fans adamantly enjoy.

"*And that's a fact!*"

Single Spotlight: "Tonight"

Def Leppard's "Tonight" single was released in March 1993.

The song was the fifth U.S. single off of the band's multi-platinum *Adrenalize* album.

Here is a cardboard insert/cut-out that Def Leppard's record company used to promote the "Tonight" single release inside CD bins back in 1993:

Wantin', Willin', Touchin'... The Charts

"Tonight" is beloved by some Def Leppard fans, captivated by the song's fervent mood and sultry lyrics. Yet others consider the track to be one of their *least* favorite ballads residing in the band's repertoire. Based on its chart performance, mainstream radio stations (and their listeners) favored the latter opinion.

The track peaked at only #62 on *Billboard*'s Hot 100 singles chart -- after only 5 weeks into its run -- which wasn't typical for a Def Leppard single at that time. (For comparison, the *Adrenalize* ballad "Have You Ever Needed Someone So Bad" peaked at #12.)

Furthermore, "Tonight" wasn't included on Def Leppard's "greatest hits" releases *Vault* or *Rock of Ages: The Definitive Collection*; it finally made the cut on *The Story So Far*, but only for the deluxe edition version.

The Music Video

The "Tonight" music video is dark -- figuratively and literally. Filmed in black and white, the video also features quick cuts of the band performing, with the footage overly contrasted to the point that band members' faces are mostly washed out at times.

It's unfortunate because the creative direction and overall presentation could have *enhanced* the song instead of *detracting* from it. Think for a moment about the "Pour Some Sugar On Me" concert music video and how its live, sold-out arena setting adds a whole new layer of energy to the viewing experience, or the unforgettable "Photograph" music video and the Marilyn Monroe character storyline that instantly comes to mind.

Those music videos *complemented* their respective songs

and had a lasting impact, leaving an unforgettable impression on Def Leppard fans.

On the other hand, the music video for "Tonight" seems excessively preoccupied with telling a brooding nighttime tale in a very, very dark forest, thus leaving disenchanted fans wanting more. A lot more.

Artistically, the visuals are relatively interesting. Commercially, though, not so much.

A Different Time, A Different Industry

It's important to note that these were trying times for the band. Aside from kicking off a whole new era due to Steve Clark's death, grunge music was quickly transforming the music industry in ways that were unfavorable and challenging to Def Leppard's brand of music.

That being said, "Tonight" was *Adrenalize*'s fifth U.S. single, and regardless of the strategic intent by the band's record company, choosing to release *another* sleekly produced ballad likely worked against Def Leppard; after all, "Have You Ever Needed Someone So Bad" and "Stand Up (Kick Love Into Motion)" had already been released as singles off the album.

A different approach for *Adrenalize*'s singles might have worked in the album's favor and further extended its chart life, but, to be fair, the erratic music industry at the time would have made things difficult no matter what course was taken.

In retrospect, the band admittedly has a lot of mixed feelings about *Adrenalize* and, arguably, the overproduction of its songs.

Years after its release, Rick Savage spoke candidly about it:

> *"We ended up making a record by the numbers... We tried to outdo 'Hysteria,' which was a mistake...It doesn't really cut it for me."*

Joe Elliott reflected on the album as well:

"My opinion of the album changes depending on which way the wind's blowing. I mean, sometimes I really don't like it, and then there's other times I think 'No, that's our glam rock album, we made a really cool record.'"

Final Thoughts

Def Leppard performed "Tonight" during the *Adrenalize* tour, but hasn't since, which is quite telling. Additionally, even though the band made it a point to perform some of their "deeper tracks" during their Las Vegas Planet Hollywood "Sin City" residency, "Tonight" *still* wasn't included.

As for whether "Tonight" is one of Def Leppard's most or least potent power ballads is open to debate. But to borrow from the song's lyrics: *If it pleases you*, well, then that's all that matters!

Single Spotlight: "Promises"

Def Leppard's "Promises" single was released in the U.S. in May 1999. (The U.K. release was July 1999.)

The track is also included in two of the band's greatest hits releases: *Rock of Ages: The Definitive Collection* and *The Story So Far* (2-CD version only).

"Promises" could very well be considered Def Leppard's return to form following a short-lived creative detour by way of the band's previous album, *Slang*.

In other words, "Promises" is Def Leppard being, well, Def Leppard.

Let's take an in-depth look back.

Promises Made

By 1999, the grunge movement, which practically tormented Def Leppard's brand of music for the majority of the decade, had run its course. Ironically, part of what made the grunge phenomenon such a powerful force as an alternative to the corporate mainstream was also what contributed to its demise, as it, too, ended up becoming a mainstream corporate product.

As grunge dissipated from Top 40 stations' airwaves, popular music redefined itself once again, this time going in a *com-*

pletely different direction, led by the likes of Britney Spears, the Backstreet Boys, and NSYNC.

Over three years had passed since Def Leppard released *Slang*, arguably the most un-Leppard-like sounding album the band ever recorded. It quickly came and went from a sales standpoint, which wasn't all that shocking, considering even Def Leppard joked that the album should have been titled "Commercial Suicide."

With the darker days of the grunge era now behind them, though, and the return of a more cheery, pop music trend emerging in their favor, what better time for Def Leppard to release another new album!

Promises Kept

The time was ripe for Def Leppard to revisit their arsenal of harmonies and hooks, all tightly wrapped within a big, slick production, and quench their fans' years-long thirst for feel-good, melodic songs. More specifically, for Def Leppard to do what they do best.

The end result was *Euphoria*, an album some would argue is the worthy successor to *Hysteria*, even more so than *Hysteria*'s actual follow-up, *Adrenalize*.

This brings us to "Promises," the song selected as the all-important first single to launch the *Euphoria* album. The song was co-written by Phil Collen and Robert John "Mutt" Lange, Def Leppard's pseudo-sixth member. (Mutt hadn't contributed as a songwriter since the band's *Adrenalize* release.)

"Promises" recaptured the radio-friendly harmonies the band frequently enjoyed in years past, with a refreshed take on their trademark sound for the new millennium.

This was essential, as it's important to keep in mind how much had changed for the band over the past decade: the glorious, chart-topping days of *Hysteria* were long gone; Steve

Clark was no longer a song contributor due to his tragic death; *Adrenalize* didn't include guitar contributions from newest member Vivian Campbell; *Slang* was a considerable departure from Def Leppard's "typical" sound.

So *Euphoria,* on the back of "Promises," was truly the first opportunity for the band's latest lineup (i.e., with Vivian Campbell) to return to and showcase Def Leppard's signature sound.

Single Strategy

"Promises" accomplished effectively launching *Euphoria* and, more importantly, relaunching the Def Leppard brand.

The song performed admirably on *Billboard*'s secondary U.S. charts -- the Hot Mainstream Rock Chart (reaching #1) and Mainstream Top 40 (peaking at #38) -- but it failed to even make it onto *Billboard*'s most prominent one, the Hot 100 singles chart. A disappointing outcome, especially for a band who regularly appeared on, if not ruled, the chart back in the days of *Pyromania, Hysteria,* and, to an extent, *Adrenalize.*

The performance of the "Promises" single was a bit of a letdown to the band, too:

> "'Promises' should have been a hit and '21st Century Sha La La La Girl,' stuff like that. They were great and had they been done in a slightly different time or environment, I think they would have been bigger songs."
> -- Phil Collen, *Songfacts.com*

> "It's a little difficult with the radio aspect. Radio is changing to a certain degree, but the first single [Promises] hasn't really kicked in the way we thought it was going to."
> -- Rick Allen, *Music Morsels Magazine*

"Promises" not being a bona fide hit single doesn't negate the fact that it helped position *Euphoria* for a strong launch, though.

Charting in the late '90s was vastly different than the '80s. Music trends weren't the only things that had changed; chart trends and performance did as well, which is why that type of data became increasingly less important with each subsequent Def Leppard release.

When "Promises" was officially released, references were made that compared it to "Photograph," which was rather unfair in setting expectations. Understandably, this was done to position the track positively and promote *Euphoria*'s release, but it was unrealistic to expect "Promises" to perform as well as one of Def Leppard's most iconic songs.

Nevertheless, that type of comparison provided Def Leppard's record company with an opportunity to solicit pop radio stations that hadn't played new music from the band in years and encourage them to reconsider. The sales pitch was compelling, along the lines of: *"Promises" has "hit single" written all over it! It features Def Leppard's classic sound, Mutt Lange is involved, and it will remind you of "Photograph." Forget Slang and Adrenalize, think Pyromania and Hysteria!*

In the end, for a band that had to withstand nearly a decade of their music becoming much less popular, the amount of radio airplay "Promises" ended up receiving was respectable.

The Music Video

The "Promises" music video's concept is similar to numerous other Def Leppard videos, balancing the band's performance footage with a secondary storyline, this time featuring an audience enjoying a 3-D planetary light show at the Griffith Observatory in Los Angeles.

The band's footage interacts well with the video's light show narrative, though a few too many edits back and forth between the two, along with an abundance of strobe lighting and other visual effects, becomes a bit distracting.

Ultimately, there isn't anything wrong with the video's concept, but fans sometimes just want to see the band straight-up perform, and they don't need unnecessary special effects to take center stage.

Final Thoughts

"Promises" did a commendable job reintroducing the type of music many Def Leppard fans had longed for, and, frankly, expected from the band.

The song also effectively served its purpose as *Euphoria*'s first single. It's a major reason why the album ended up selling nearly 100,000 copies (just over 98,000) in the U.S. in its first week of release. (The album went on to achieve gold certification status, with sales exceeding 500,000 copies.)

"Promises" put Def Leppard back on a path to do what initially brought the band great success: providing listeners with music escapism via feel-good songs overflowing with hooks and melodies. It also periodically makes an appearance on Def Leppard's tours, pleasantly surprising audiences, especially those yearning for a bit of a shake-up to the band's setlist.

To this day, "Promises" remains one of the band's "newer" classics, delivering the pleasing-to-the-ear harmonies Def Leppard fans crave.

That's a promise.

Single Spotlight: "Long Long Way To Go"

Def Leppard's "Long Long Way To Go" single was released in April 2003.

It may be surprising to some, but this sentimental favorite is not included in *any* of Def Leppard's U.S. greatest hits releases. (It was only part of the band's limited edition 2004 "Best Of" U.K. release.)

"Long Long Way To Go" isn't your typical Def Leppard power ballad, though, for various reasons. Let's take an in-depth look back and see why!

Long, Long Way To... Reprising Chart Success

If you've already read some of the other chapters in this book that spotlight a Def Leppard song or album, you're likely accustomed to seeing at least *some* chart performance analysis. Well, this is *not* one of those times, because "Long Long Way To Go" failed to even make it onto *Billboard*'s Hot 100 singles chart in the U.S. (It *barely* cracked the Top 40 in the U.K., peaking at #40.)

This shouldn't be that surprising, though, as the chart performance of Def Leppard's singles lost most of their meaning after the band's *Adrenalize* release. That being said, it doesn't mean the single's release *strategy* cannot be revisited!

The decision was made to release "Now" -- an absolutely solid track, but arguably more of a deep cut -- as the *X* album's all-important lead-off single. To be clear, that's not to say "Long Long Way To Go" should have taken its place. But there were stronger options.

This all goes back to the unfortunate approach taken to market and promote the *X* album. (See the *X* chapter for much more on that.)

Case in point, the *X* album was released in July 2002; "Long Long Way To Go" was released as a single in April 2003, *eight months* after the album's release. By then, *X*'s awareness and sales momentum were long, long gone.

So not having "Long Long Way To Go" appear on *Billboard*'s Hot 100 U.S. singles chart is not at all shocking.

A Different Kind Of Def Leppard Ballad

There are certainly opposing views from fans about "Long Long Way To Go" (and the *X* album, for that matter).

On one end of the spectrum, some consider "Long Long Way To Go" one of Def Leppard's quintessential ballads, heartfelt and emotional; on the other end, some adamantly believe the song (as well as *X*) is excessively poppy and verges into "boy band" territory.

Regardless of your stance, both opinions can simultaneously apply.

"Long Long Way To Go" is one of those rare instances where Def Leppard was *not* involved in writing the song, not even in a co-writing capacity. It was written by Wayne Hector and Steve Robson, songwriters who enjoyed enormous songwriting success with numerous multi-platinum acts, including One Direction, Christina Aguilera, and Pink, among others.

Just because Def Leppard didn't write "Long Long Way To Go" doesn't mean it isn't a quality ballad, regardless of which era of the band you prefer. It strikes a chord (no pun intended) with many fans, and its emotional themes of loss and coping are effective. So much so, opinions can vary widely as to what the song's lyrics are *really* about: The break-up of a relationship? The loss of a loved one? Subtle references included throughout about the band's loss of Steve Clark?

Open interpretations allow for fans to personally connect with the song any way they please, just the way it should be.

An Even Longer Way To Go

"Long Long Way To Go" never truly received the recognition it deserved.

As mentioned, the *X* album's promotional strategy was nowhere near as effective as it could have been, but, to be fair, the latter part of the '90s and early 2000s weren't very kind to the band, and their popularity took a hit, thanks in large part to the grunge music era.

"Long Long Way To Go" isn't necessarily the "go-to" power ballad on the *X* album either, as it resides among other adult contemporary-like tracks that could also fit the bill, unlike previous albums.

For instance, *High 'n' Dry* had "Bringin' On The Heartbreak," *Hysteria* had "Love Bites," *Adrenalize* had "Have You Ever Needed Someone So Bad," and so on. In contrast, *X* had "Long Long Way To Go," "Let Me Be The One," and the underrated "Unbelievable" (which, ironically, also wasn't written by any member of Def Leppard). So "Long Long Way To Go" was just one of a handful of ballad offerings.

Would a song like "Long Long Way To Go" have had more success and notoriety if it had been included on *Hysteria* or *Adrenalize*? Almost certainly. Would other tracks like "Torn To

Shreds," "Everyday," or "Unbelievable" have been good single options for the X album, in addition to "Long Long Way To Go"? Most likely. In hindsight, would it have made a huge difference? Maybe, maybe not.

In the end, "Long Long Way To Go" was one of the very few singles chosen to represent and (belatedly) promote the X album, and the song didn't catch on. (It did grab the attention of Lionel Richie, though, who ended up recording his own version of the song in 2004, so at least there's that.)

The Music Video

The "Long Long Way To Go" music video featured subtle mood lighting, a candle-filled set, and saturated colors which all matched up well with the song's somber themes and the band's toned-down performance.

The music video would have worked just as well without the obscure storyline periodically wedged into the band's performance footage, particularly unnecessary shots focusing on a mouse scurrying around the floor.

Most unfortunate, though, was no longer having a reliable promotional outlet like MTV to air and support "Long Long Way To Go." As a result, many potential fans missed out on discovering the song, and, ultimately, the X album.

Final Thoughts

Similar to "Tonight," "Long Long Way To Go" had its moment in time, albeit a very brief one.

Def Leppard performed the song during their X tour, just like when they performed "Tonight" on the *Adrenalize* tour, but once touring wrapped up in support of each of those albums, so did setlist inclusion for those songs going forward.

"Long Long Way To Go" wasn't even included in the band's

well-received live, nearly 8-minute "acoustic medley" (also released digitally in 2012), even though it would have fit right in. (Ironically, the *X* track "Now" did make it into the acoustic jam.)

"Long Long Way To Go" might not reside near the top of some fans' lists of favorite Def Leppard power ballads, but its solid arrangement, heartfelt lyrics, rich lead vocals, and infectious melodies go a long, long way, and are worth revisiting and appreciating.

Single Spotlight: "Nine Lives"

Def Leppard's "Nine Lives" U.S. single was released in April 2008.

The song featured a collaboration with country music superstar Tim McGraw and was chosen as the lead single from the band's *Songs from the Sparkle Lounge* album. (The track is also included on the band's *The Story So Far* greatest hits album.)

"Nine Lives" is an unconventional Def Leppard song and isn't among the band's top chart performers -- actually, it didn't even make it onto *Billboard*'s Hot 100 singles chart.

But "Nine Lives" achieved one very important goal as only it could: garnering plenty of publicity for its unique rock and country music alliance while hyping the release of *Songs from the Sparkle Lounge*.

Took A Chance On A Chance... And A Song Was Born

Tim McGraw co-wrote "Nine Lives" with Def Leppard (specifically Phil Collen, Joe Elliott, and Rick Savage).

Tim described the experience of working with the band to CMT.com:

"Each of us brought something different to the table, and we drew on each other's influence to finish it out. They are simply one of the best rock bands ever, and it was a great time working together."

How did the collaboration come to be? Tim McGraw's tour manager was none other than Robert Allen (Rick Allen's brother), and with Tim being such a big fan of Def Leppard's music, the pieces quickly fell into place.

Joe Elliott elaborated on the joint effort to Billboard.com in 2008:

"We've kind of known Tim and [his wife] Faith Hill are huge Leppard fans and have been for many years. When we played the Hollywood Bowl in 2006, Tim happened to be in L.A., so we invited him down; it was one of those, "Hey, man, you want to get up and do something?" So we did "Pour Some Sugar on Me," which went down really well.

"We had a good laugh that night and lo and behold, when we came through Nashville just a short while later, he came down to soundcheck and we ended up in the Sparkle Lounge, and that's where the song was conceived."

The final result is a song that primarily showcases Def Leppard's rock roots, yet has Tim McGraw's country music vibe sprinkled in throughout.

Joe Elliott also shared his thoughts on whether the song is more rock or country:

"People have been bringing that question up: 'You guys have gone country?' 'No! Tim went rock!' And truth be

known, that's really what he did. If you listen to the record, he goes off on his own kind of twangy tangent for the beginning part, but after that, even me and him could barely distinguish one from another... So he really stepped up to the plate in the rock sense."

Welcome To Def Leppard Country

Def Leppard made a noteworthy push into the world of country music in 2008, which provided the band with the opportunity to further expand its fan base.

And why not? The band's music had already crossed over beyond straight-up rock, and their influence on other artists validated how far-reaching their appeal was across genres. Just ask self-proclaimed Def Leppard fans Lady Gaga, Pink, Maroon 5, Mariah Carey, Jewel, Allison Krauss, John Mayer, and so on.

Country music superstar Taylor Swift, a huge Def Leppard fan, performed with the band in an episode of "CMT Crossroads," also released in 2008, the same year as "Nine Lives."

And to connect some random events for your amusement:

> 1. Taylor Swift's first-ever published song was titled "Tim McGraw";
>
> 2. Def Leppard and Taylor Swift performed together on "CMT Crossroads";
>
> 3. Def Leppard recorded "Nine Lives" with Tim McGraw;
>
> 4. When Rick Savage joined his daughter for her live singing debut at 2010's Dave Kilner tribute concert in Sheffield, the two of them performed the song "Tim McGraw" by Taylor Swift.

Round and round we go!

The Music Video

Directed by the late Sherman Halsey, the "Nine Lives" music video interspersed black & white footage with grainy, washed-out performance footage, and vibrant, over-saturated color performance footage.

Even though the briskly paced editing and interwoven black & white vs. color footage are somewhat overdone and distracting, the video ultimately captured the spirit of the project: everyone involved having a really good time.

Final Thoughts

"Nine Lives" is a bit rough around the edges, which is likely intentional, at least to an extent, to achieve a more "raw" result than your typical slickly produced Def Leppard song. But, frankly, that carries the track only so far, as its shouted *"Nine Lives! Nine Times To Die!"* chorus doesn't quite flow off the tongue so easily or reach the satiating levels of melody fans normally expect from the band.

Arguably, there were stronger song options to launch *Songs from the Sparkle Lounge*, such as "C'mon C'mon" (as a lead-off single), or "Go" or "Tomorrow" (for album-oriented rock stations), but "Nine Lives" served its purpose by attracting added attention to the album for the band to capitalize on, at least for a little while.

Similar to other short-lived Def Leppard singles -- "Tonight" and "Long Long Way To Go" are two examples -- "Nine Lives" received concert setlist inclusion for a brief period, primarily with the intent of promoting the *Songs from the Sparkle Lounge* release on the album's tour.

In all likelihood, "Nine Lives" won't have a recurring slot on future Def Leppard tour setlists, which is more a testament to the strength and depth of the band's catalog rather than how well the track has aged over the years.

Plain and simple, "Nine Lives" is a solid, flat-out rocker. It's also a fitting title for Def Leppard and the seemingly insurmountable odds the band has had to overcome throughout its career. As the lyric goes, *"Are you tough enough, is your stuff enough?"* Many would agree when it comes to Def Leppard, the answer is most definitely yes.

The Magical Mysteria Of "Mutt" Lange

The name Robert John "Mutt" Lange can evoke a variety of spirited thoughts and passionate opinions, primarily driven by his large body of work as a record producer and songwriter.

For some, Mutt Lange is known simply as "Shania Twain's ex-husband," which is a shame, as it overlooks his immense contributions to her career, not to mention the music industry.

It's no coincidence that Mutt Lange was married to Shania Twain during her most successful years as a recording artist. That's not to say Shania didn't enjoy some success on her own, albeit on a much smaller scale, before marrying and working with "Mutt" -- her self-titled debut album (aka pre-Mutt Lange) did reach platinum certification status, selling one million copies.

As for Shania's subsequent albums, in which Mutt Lange was heavily involved: *The Woman In Me* achieved 12x platinum certification -- *twelve million* copies sold. Hit songs off the album such as "No One Needs To Know," "Whose Bed Have Your Boots Been Under?," and "Any Man Of Mine" were *all* co-written and produced by Mutt Lange.

Shania's third album, *Come On Over*, went 21x platinum in the U.S. alone -- selling *over 40 million copies* worldwide -- and remains one of the biggest selling albums of all time. Hit songs included "Don't Be Stupid (You Know I Love You)," "You're Still The One," "That Don't Impress Me Much," "Man! I Feel Like A

Woman" -- again, *all* co-written and produced by Mutt Lange.

Moreover, Mutt Lange's unmistakable, signature backing vocals are heard throughout the album's meticulously polished production, so much so that one can perhaps misconstrue Shania Twain's song "Honey, I'm Home" as featuring Def Leppard as the backing band -- just throw in some country music flair to go with those anthemic "Pour Some Sugar On Me"-like *Hey!* chants.

Shania's follow-up album *Up* continued her multi-platinum streak, achieving 11x platinum. Infectious, radio-friendly songs like "Up," "I'm Gonna Getcha Good," "Ka-Ching" helped propel the album's success, along with tracks like "Nah," another tune with the familiar makings and sound of a Def Leppard music production.

All three of these mega-successful Shania Twain albums featured enormous, glossy productions and melodic songs packed with inescapable hooks and irresistible harmonies. Sound familiar, Def Leppard fans? But make no mistake: the music was *not* Def Leppard-like. The songs were Mutt Lange creations, painstakingly crafted to showcase Shania Twain's style of country music precisely through Mutt's methodical hitmaking prism, which unabashedly includes his own unmistakable backing vocals and unforgettable choruses.

In short, it's Mutt Lange being "Mutt," one of the most successful record producers and songwriters in music history.

That's who Mutt Lange is.

The Mutt Lange Effect

Mutt Lange's collaboration with Shania Twain ended in 2010, coinciding with the end of their marriage. Since the dissolution of their relationship, and after an extended hiatus away from the spotlight, Shania released her first and only post-Mutt Lange studio album titled *Now* in 2017.

To this day, the album's sales *still* haven't reached platinum status in the U.S. Not even gold.

Calling out this underperformance is not meant to disparage Shania Twain's talents, but it undeniably shines a bright light on what a difference-maker Mutt Lange is, and the magnitude of success and crossover appeal he can bring to an artist's career. And it endures: Shania's post-Mutt 2012-2014 Las Vegas concert residency was titled *Still The One* and featured a setlist comprised of almost all Mutt Lange-era songs from her catalog; the same goes for the vast majority of the setlist from her 2019 *Let's Go!* Vegas residency.

Shania Twain is but one example. Some of music's biggest, most iconic albums and songs are the direct result of Mutt Lange's involvement and exceptional, hitmaking abilities. And while many are likely aware of *some* of his work, they might also be surprised to discover how extensive and far-reaching it is. In fact, with a career that has spanned nearly fifty years, it's plausible that some of your favorite songs over the past few decades involved Mutt Lange.

Def Leppard's Sixth Member

Mutt Lange has often been referred to as the unofficial sixth member of Def Leppard because of the immense amount of influence he's had on the band's career.

Mutt's collaboration with the boys from Sheffield didn't begin until *High 'n' Dry*, the first album he produced for the band. *Pyromania* followed, chock-full of classic rock songs like "Photograph," "Rock of Ages," and "Foolin'" -- all co-written and produced by Mutt Lange (in addition to every other song on the album). Colossal album sales resulted, as did a more mature, well-crafted Def Leppard sound that appealed to the masses.

"Mutt's one of the best producers in rock. Most producers

can't explain something from a musician's point of view. But Mutt is a trained musician himself. He can change an arrangement around if it's not right... When you're working with Mutt -- and a lot of guys will tell you this -- you come out of the studio a better musician."
-- Steve Clark, Rock Fever magazine

Then came mega-successful *Hysteria*, an album whose original song creations were mostly shelved, with several of them included on the band's *Retro Active* release. Why? Because after several unsuccessful starts, *Hysteria* was completely overhauled when Mutt Lange joined the project.

Joe Elliott discussed Mutt reuniting with the band in an interview with RollingStone.com:

> "We were like this rudderless ship without Mutt producing it. But once he came in, everybody's focus went in and we started throwing new ideas in, and all the better songs came about."

Mutt Lange steered the proverbial Def Leppard ship around and into a completely different musical direction, with the clear intent of creating a rock album equivalent to Michael Jackson's *Thriller*, brimming with radio-friendly hit singles.

> "Mutt said, 'Look, everyone else is copying 'Pyromania,' so we don't want to make 'Pyromania 2.' We should do a rock version of Michael Jackson's 'Thriller,' where it crosses over.' That was the role model that we wanted to use. We wanted to make a hybrid." -- Phil Collen

One of the *Hysteria* project's biggest and most extraordinary obstacles was Rick Allen's tragic car accident. The unfathomable challenge of a drummer losing an arm was undoubtedly uncharted territory, and could easily have ended his drumming career.

Fortunately, as a result of a whole new mindset and approach to drumming which utilized his remaining limbs, and *a lot* of hard work, Rick not only triumphed but thrived, reinventing himself as a musician and inspiring millions along the way. Much easier said than done, though, as such an endeavor offered no guarantee of success and a whole lot of uncertainty.

Rick struggled with the situation and nearly gave up at the outset, if not for the help of Mutt Lange.

> *"There were times at the beginning when I really felt like I couldn't do this anymore. The thing that really helped is Mutt came to visit and he talked me into being able to do this [drumming] but in a different way."* -- Rick Allen

> *"I remember when Steve [Clark] and I first went to see [Rick] in the hospital how terrible it was. We both thought, There's no way he's going to be able to do this again...But you know, Mutt's actually great about that kind of stuff, too. He told Rick, 'Why don't you get some pedals and other things and just play?' And Rick said, 'Well, no one's done it.' And Mutt responded, 'Then you'd be the first.'"*
> -- Phil Collen, Guitar World magazine

Mutt Lange's influence and overall impact on Def Leppard went far beyond songwriting and studio wizardry. The band not only utilized but *embraced* his guidance and expertise, placing their faith in him to create the album *he* envisioned, even as his grandiose plan seemed so unambiguous to them initially.

> *"Mutt was able to put himself in a situation where he could imagine every single instrument that was going to be played on the ['Hysteria'] record. He had a vision that I don't think any of us got at first. His vision was so clear and he'd stop at nothing to get what he wanted."* -- Rick Allen

This harkens back to when Mutt Lange saw untapped potential in Def Leppard after the release of their debut album *On Through The Night* and believed he could help elevate the young, up-and-coming band to greater heights. *High 'n' Dry* resulted, an album some fans believe showcases Def Leppard at their best.

Mutt Lange's *High 'n' Dry* production featured a tighter, more sleek sound compared to *On Through The Night*, denoted in rockers like "Another Hit and Run," "You Got Me Runnin'," and "Mirror, Mirror (Look Into My Eyes)," as well as "Bringin' on the Heartbreak," which introduced a somewhat softer side to the band's music.

The made-for-TV movie *Hysteria: The Def Leppard Story* -- a guilty pleasure for some -- included a scene featuring an interaction in the recording studio between Joe Elliott's character (or "caricature," as Joe later called it) and Mutt Lange (played by Anthony Michael Hall) which provided a *very* small, intriguing glimpse into Mutt Lange's influence and overall vision for Def Leppard.

The scene embodied how Mutt Lange continually pushed the band to ultimately exceed *their own* expectations.

> *"[Mutt Lange's] an inspiration to be around. You'd try something and he'd always have great ideas and he'd go, 'Try this!' You go, 'I can't really play that.' He'd go, 'Yeah, just do it.' He would get you to sing stuff that was above*

your level. He'd go, 'Okay, just try it.' I'd go, 'I can't hit that note.' He'd say, 'Yeah, you can!' Just the vocal alone, he'd go, 'No, it sounds great. Just try it! Alright, we got it. Now double-track it.' Before you know it, you're in there and your new bar has been raised. He was amazing like that."
-- Phil Collen, Guitar Interactive magazine

Def Leppard and Mutt Lange's collaborative success with *High 'n' Dry* brought about *Pyromania*, where he took an even greater role in constructing, far beyond producing. For example, aside from Joe Elliott, Mutt Lange is the only other person credited as a songwriter on every one of *Pyromania*'s tracks.

Pyromania introduced fans to "Def Leppard 2.0" -- an arena rock band whose finely crafted commercial sound, enriched with bountiful backing vocals (including Mutt's), would ultimately become Def Leppard's hallmark and an essential component of its success.

Def Leppard's rough-around-the-edges, hard rock sound had transformed. *Pyromania*'s songs still packed a wallop but were much more radio-friendly. "Photograph" became the band's first Top 20 single in the U.S., just missing the Top 10. "Rock of Ages" and "Foolin'" also filled radio airwaves and made their mark, not to take anything away from the album's classic deep cuts -- tracks like "Too Late for Love," "Billy's Got A Gun," and "Rock! Rock! (Till You Drop)" to name a few -- which may not have been official singles but were just as vital in making the album a 10x platinum-selling powerhouse.

It's worth noting that Def Leppard also replaced guitarist Pete Willis with Phil Collen during the recording of *Pyromania*. According to Joe Elliott, the decision to hire Phil ultimately required the final blessing of one person: Mutt Lange. That's how integral his guidance and influence was to Def Leppard, and how much trust the band put in him.

"The important thing was that Phil and Mutt got on well. They met up at Battery Studios in London, and after hearing him play a solo for Stagefright, 'Mutt' said, 'Sign him up!'"
-- Joe Elliott, Record Collector magazine

Bringin' On The 'Hysteria'

This brings us to *Hysteria*, Def Leppard's most successful, best-selling album.

Once again, Mutt Lange's hard-driving, ambitious approach -- at times even recording the most subtle guitar tracks one note at a time -- is evident throughout the album.

Going exceedingly beyond the role of record producer -- and this is where the moniker of being the unofficial sixth member of Def Leppard especially takes hold -- Mutt Lange co-wrote *every* song on the iconic album. Backing vocals also included Mutt's distinct voice, sometimes prominently.

One example is the album's title track "Hysteria" and its infectious *"Oh, can you feel it? Do you believe it?"* chorus. Those multi-layered backing vocals showcase Mutt Lange's voice, an essential part of what makes it sound the way it does. On one hand, unique -- it's Def Leppard's "trademark sound." But in a broader sense, it's Mutt Lange's recording process and formula in action. It's a technique you've likely heard elsewhere numerous times. (More on that in a moment.)

"Mutt sings on everything he's ever done with [Def Leppard]. And he's an amazing singer... On Hysteria, he basically said that we needed to make the backing vocals sound like another instrument." -- Phil Collen, Guitar World

The genius of Mutt Lange's hitmaking abilities is also evident when revisiting the origins of the song "Hysteria," a track which Phil Collen and Rick Savage *initially thought* had a chorus...until Mutt Lange intervened.

Phil explains:

> "It started off, we were in Dublin and Rick Savage started playing this tune, so I immediately started singing, 'Out of touch, out of reach.' That was literally the first thing that came out of my mouth. He said that was cool and he goes, [singing] 'I got to know tonight,' this whole other section. We glued it together and we got very excited... We sat down and were playing acoustic guitar, singing over the demo, and we thought that was going to be the chorus. And Mutt Lange said, 'Okay, that's a great verse, a great bridge. Now we need the chorus.' Uh, okay. [Laughs]"

Hysteria ballad "Love Bites" ended up being Def Leppard's first (and only) #1 single. Where did the song originate? Mutt Lange. As for the song's catchy, unforgettable backing vocals, which showcase that oh-so-familiar *Hysteria* album multi-layered sound? Phil confirms:

> "['Love Bites'] was really a Mutt Lange song - he brought it to us and he played it on an acoustic guitar to me and Steve... Most of the backing vocals on that song are actually Mutt singing. We are on there but you can't really hear us - that's all Mutt's vocals."

Revisit the chorus on tracks like "Hysteria" (*"Oh, can you feel it? Do you believe* it?!") and "Love Bites" (*"Love bites! Love bleeds!"*). The harmonies are *so* Mutt Lange.

Mutt Lange's significant importance to Def Leppard's success is further exemplified with *Hysteria*'s biggest, most iconic track, and the one that catapulted the album's (and band's) popularity into the stratosphere: "Pour Some Sugar On Me"

Joe Elliott was fooling around on an acoustic guitar during a break from recording his vocals for "Armageddon It," and he came up with a guitar hook idea consisting of three chords, spontaneously adding in *"Pour some sugar on me"* as a lyric.

While it could easily have been dismissed as a mere guitar exercise to pass the time, it was Mutt Lange who overheard Joe's impromptu hook and insisted the idea be pursued further, ultimately envisioning yet another track for the *Hysteria* album. This was *after* the album was considered complete with a total of eleven songs; "Pour Some Sugar On Me" would be a *very* late addition and its unexpected twelfth track.

Rick Savage put "Sugar's" importance into perspective in an interview with MusicRadar.com:

> *"It all happened because Mutt Lange heard something there that the album didn't have."*

Part of the song's appeal was its distinct rap-like verses, an idea conceived by Mutt Lange.

> *"When we started writing the song, Mutt said it should almost be like a rap song."*
> -- Phil Collen

And those monstrous, unforgettable guitar riffs throughout the track?

> *"Mutt actually came up with that 'Pour Some Sugar On Me' riff. He's a country fan, so he was playing it with his fingers...I use a metal pick, so that was my interpretation."*

-- Phil Collen

Hysteria would sell over 15 million copies in the U.S. alone, matching and *far* surpassing the sales of *Pyromania*, and Def Leppard would become one of only five bands in music history to achieve diamond certification (over 10 million albums sold) on back-to-back album releases. This feat is yet another example of Mutt Lange's impact on Def Leppard, and also a reaffirmation of the success, if not magic, that ensues when they collaborate.

Recording a rock album packed with numerous hit singles to counter Michael Jackson's *Thriller* may have been considered unrealistic and foolish initially, but it was Mutt Lange's vision from the start, and it's exactly what he and the band achieved with *Hysteria*. That said, it's not an overstatement to say that the album wouldn't have reached the level of success it did without "Pour Some Sugar On Me," an idea that was pursued at Mutt's insistence, and a song that became one of the '80s biggest and most iconic rock anthems.

"I think without Mutt's vision the [Hysteria] record would have been a more standard-sounding thing. He definitely pushed it."
-- Phil Collen, Guitar World

In recent years, Phil has spoken further about Mutt Lange's immeasurable contributions to *Hysteria* and the band:

"That whole album, [Mutt] really taught us how to sing and play. I think we'd been an okay band, we'd been a good band, but he made it something great. He deserves all the credit."

Mutt Lange And Def Leppard

Mutt Lange left an indelible mark on Def Leppard's path to stardom, and even though he didn't officially produce any more of the band's albums after *Hysteria*, his presence and influence still lingered.

Def Leppard's follow-up album *Adrenalize*, the band's first without guitarist Steve Clark, listed Mutt Lange as a co-writer on every song (including biggest hits "Let's Get Rocked" and "Have You Ever Needed Someone So Bad") but one, older track "Tear It Down."

He also contributed backing vocals, which helped maintain a sense of familiarity to the songs' multi-layered choruses which fans fondly remembered from *Hysteria*. His creative input remained vital as well. For instance, Phil Collen penned an early version of the song that would become "Have You Ever Needed Someone So Bad." In Phil's original arrangement, the opening verse began with the lyric "*Have you ever needed someone so bad.*" Mutt Lange recommended making that line the song's chorus instead; he also ended up creating the ballad's memorable bridge.

Nevertheless, Mutt Lange's work on *Adrenalize* was nowhere near as extensive as *Hysteria*, but out of respect for his contributions, the band still credited him as executive producer.

Adrenalize did mark a transition in the working relationship between Def Leppard and Mutt Lange, as it was the start of a much more limited and diminished role in the band's projects going forward.

Future Def Leppard albums sporadically included Mutt Lange's involvement, typically resulting in a single-worthy track tailor-made for radio airplay. Case in point, after going down a less commercial path with the album *Slang*, the band's desire to return to a more mainstream-sounding release -- i.e., something more true to form for Def Leppard -- resulted in *Euphoria*, an album whose first and most successful single was fan-favorite "Promises," a song co-written by Mutt Lange.

The band's follow-up album *X* involved outside songwriters in hopes of delivering "the goods" and rekindling chart success, but it didn't involve Mutt Lange. The album, for various reasons, severely underperformed and didn't feature *any* singles that were deemed "hits" on the *Billboard* charts.

Subsequent studio album *Songs from the Sparkle Lounge* -- which includes a photo of Mutt Lange on its *Sgt. Pepper*-ish cover -- was initially going to include a collaboration with him, but it didn't pan out. 2015's self-titled *Def Leppard* album did not involve Mutt Lange either.

Who Is Mutt Lange?

Aside from all his work with Def Leppard, Mutt Lange has played an integral role in creating some of music's most popular songs for decades.

Even early on in his career as a record producer in the mid-'70s, his involvement in projects would be a harbinger of things to come. 1978's song "Rat Trap" by Bob Geldof's band The Boomtown Rats, produced by Mutt, reached #1 on the U.K. charts. The feat also marked the first time an Irish band, not to mention a new wave song, topped the British charts.

Another example is the little-known U.K. band City Boy. Mutt Lange produced several albums for the group, but his contributions extended well beyond the role of producer.

City Boy's bassist Chris Dunn summed up Mutt's above-and-beyond approach on the podcast "The Hustle":

> *"Mutt's method of production is kind of interesting because he will listen to your song, and he will completely dismantle it, and then put it back together again, and*

it will be nothing like it used to be but way better, of course."

Additionally, Mutt would go on to help teach the band the craft of song arrangements, even taking part in the vocal harmonies himself. One notable standout track is the engrossing, if not slightly odd, track "Dinner at the Ritz" -- off-putting for some yet unique and perhaps mesmerizing.

Mutt Lange's far-reaching involvement also included helping Chris Dunn work on improving his bass playing skills, and even going out on tour with the band to help out as their sound engineer! Over time, Mutt's extensive contributions resulted in him being considered the unofficial, seventh member of City Boy. Sound familiar, Def Leppard fans?

This would all be a springboard for a long-lasting career filled with tremendous success, with hit songs and albums abound that would transform music acts into superstars, and in the process render him one of the music industry's most consequential figures.

That's Mutt Lange.

Mutt's significance transcends beyond studio craftsmanship featuring "polished" productions. His immersion delves deep into a song's fundamental structure and overall arrangement: dissecting how its verses build and effortlessly lead into a pre-chorus and chorus to reward listeners for taking the journey, all the while placing ear-candy hooks throughout so that the song's harmonies unavoidably linger in a listener's mind long after hearing them.

While known for working with some of rock's greatest acts and Shania Twain, Mutt Lange's familiar "calling card" can also be heard throughout the work he's done with so many other artists.

Revisit the late-'80s self-titled debut album from the band Romeo's Daughter, a release which Mutt Lange co-wrote the majority of songs for and co-produced (splitting the duties with John Paar of "St. Elmo's Fire" fame). The album's most notable track, "Heaven In The Backseat," showcases all the right hooks in all the right places, particularly around its melodic chorus, but that's not the only thing that stands out. What else does? The backing vocals heard throughout the song.

By the time you reach the song's three-minute mark, and start hearing lines shouted out like "*C'mon, fire me up*!" (a familiar lyric to "Pour Some Sugar On Me" fans) and "*Body rockin'!*," you might be taken aback at just how Def Leppard-esque it sounds.

Did Def Leppard actually contribute backing vocals on the track?

Nope.

That's Mutt Lange, and it's merely one of many examples that feature his trademark sound. (Years later, Eddie Money would release his own version of "Heaven In The Backseat." When compared to the original, it's fairly easy to identify which version -- his or Romeo's Daughter -- is a Mutt Lange production, and features Mutt on background vocals.)

Mutt Lange's Trademark Sound

While some of the most popular, beloved songs from the '80s and '90s (and beyond) involved Mutt Lange, other lesser-known songs also have that instantly recognizable sound.

For example, the band Starship, known for "We Built This City" and "Sara," released a song in 1989 called "I Didn't Mean To Stay All Night":

- The opening notes bring to mind The Cars' classic song "Drive" (which Mutt Lange produced).
- The lead vocals have a striking resemblance to Bryan Adams (an artist Mutt Lange has also worked with).

- The pre-chorus *"I am flyin', forever within your arms..."* evokes memories of *"I would fight for you, I'd lie for you,"* from the blockbuster song "(Everything I Do) I Do It For You" (which Mutt Lange produced and co-wrote).
- The chorus, with its lines of *"I didn't mean!"* and *"Oh no!"* showcases a massive wall of backing vocals that sound very Def Leppard-like.

Put it all together, and it becomes abundantly clear the song is a Mutt Lange creation.

Even the chorus' structure has similarities to Def Leppard's "Love Bites," a song that originated with Mutt Lange. Lyrics *"But, baby, you hold so tight!"* and *"It's heaven, it can't be wrong..."* are performed in such a way that they harken back to and can easily be juxtaposed with Joe Elliott's classic "Love Bites" vocal line *"It's bringin' me to my knees!"*

It's not a coincidence these comparisons intertwine with other Mutt Lange songs. Neither is the fact that the co-producer of Starship's song was Mike Shipley, Mutt Lange's right-hand man on numerous projects, including Def Leppard's *High 'n' Dry*, *Pyromania*, and *Hysteria*. Many songs Mutt Lange and Mike Shipley worked on together had a larger-than-life, layered sound all its own, which is also why a "Mutt Lange song" can sound so familiar.

The late Mike Shipley touched on explaining *that* particular sound:

> *"There was a sound [to] the records in the Def Leppard era that was conceptualized between Mutt and myself... Mutt was just brilliant. There's so much depth of field to the way he produced those records in terms of the parts. The concept of how to make the drums sound and how to make the guitars sound and how to stack up hundreds of tracks of backgrounds. There were so many layers..."*

So it shouldn't be all that surprising when listening to some of Mutt Lange's music projects and thinking to yourself, "*Is this a Bryan Adams song?*" or "*This sounds just like Def Leppard,*" and so on.

In the end, Starship's song, though not a chart-topper by any means, shines a spotlight on Mutt Lange's craft and techniques, putting them on full display. Those hallmark harmonies and pleasing hooks effectively, well, hook listeners in.

Mutt Lange's X-Factor

Mutt Lange's involvement in Def Leppard's career has been well-documented in other chapters of this book, most notably highlighting the numerous challenges he helped the band overcome during the recording of the *Hysteria* album.

But another prime example where Mutt played a pivotal role in helping a band reach even greater levels of success is AC/DC. The band had already achieved some notoriety but it wasn't until he produced their sixth album, *Highway to Hell*, that their popularity soared. And similar to helping Def Leppard overcome the unfathomable challenge of drummer Rick Allen losing his arm (which resulted in recording what would be the band's biggest-selling album), Mutt also helped AC/DC deal with their own devastating situation -- the tragic death of lead singer, Bon Scott -- which led to *Back In Black*, the best-selling hard rock album of all time.

The terms "genius" and "uber-producer" are often used when describing Mutt Lange, but the fact that he was able to play such a critical role in the careers of Def Leppard and AC/DC, at some of their lowest, make-or-break moments speaks volumes about what a difference-maker he can be, and underscores how his talents go *way* beyond that of a record producer or songwriter for hire.

Mutt Lange: Hit Songs And Albums

Here are just some of the most notable songs and albums involving Mutt Lange.

AC/DC:

As monstrous as Def Leppard's combined U.S. sales certifications are for *Pyromania* and *Hysteria*, AC/DC's *Back In Black* album -- again, which Mutt Lange produced -- has sold more units than both Def Leppard albums *combined*.

Back in Black has not only been certified diamond (10x platinum, 10 million copies), it has surpassed *double diamond* certification status (25x platinum, 25 million+ copies). The album's sales have even outperformed *Come On Over*, Mutt Lange's most successful album collaboration with Shania Twain, which is certified 20x platinum.

Mutt Lange's work with AC/DC brought about the band's most iconic releases, which featured some of their most memorable, classic songs.

The three albums Mutt produced -- septuple-platinum *Highway to Hell*, quadruple-platinum *For Those About To Rock* (which was also AC/DC's first #1 album), and, of course, *Back In Black* -- have sold over 36 million copies combined!

Bryan Adams:

In addition to co-writing and producing Bryan Adams' colossal hit "Everything I Do (I Do It For You)," Mutt Lange also co-wrote the massively successful #1 single "All For Love" featuring Bryan Adams, Rod Stewart, and Sting.

Moreover, Mutt produced and co-wrote every song on Bryan Adams' album *Waking Up The Neighbours*. (This also happened to be the project he was busy working on when Def Leppard was in search of a producer for *Adrenalize*, resulting in Mike Shipley taking on the role.)

Bryan Adams' record is filled with Mutt's signature production methods and likely perks up the ears of Def Leppard fans at times. "Thought I Died And Gone To Heaven" features lead vocals that echo Joe Elliott at times, and has a chorus and bridge bursting with -- you guessed it -- multi-layered, Leppard-esque backing vocals.

It's *so* Mutt Lange.

> *"That's [Mutt's] voice you hear in back on Highway to Hell, Back in Black, the Shania Twain stuff, the Bryan Adams stuff. He can make his voice sound like anything."*
> -- Phil Collen, Guitar World

Another standout track from the album is infectious rocker "All I Want Is You." Once you surpass the song's 90-second mark, flashes of Def Leppard in your mind are understandable, particularly when hearing the line "*If you don't need love, you gotta be nuts, the heaviest metal always rusts...,*" which is performed in the same gravelly vocal spirit as Joe Elliott on "Pour Some Sugar On Me."

Mutt Lange collaborated with Bryan Adams once again on the follow-up album *18 Till I Die*, which featured yet another stand-out ballad: "Have You Ever Really Loved A Woman?" The song, co-written and co-produced by Mutt, reached #1 on *Billboard*'s Hot 100 singles chart and remained there for five consecutive weeks.

The Cars:

The Cars' 1984 quadruple-selling album *Heartbeat City* was produced by Mutt Lange. (This is the album Mutt was working on when Def Leppard was attempting to work on *Pyromania*'s follow-up, hoping to collaborate with him again. Ironically, the delays, false starts, and Rick Allen's car accident allowed for so much time to pass that Mutt was able to complete this Cars release and then return and start anew for what would become *Hysteria*.)

As for *Heartbeat City*, the album produced five Top 40 singles, including classic '80s songs "You Might Think," "Hello Again," as well as "Drive" (the band's biggest hit in the U.S.) and "Magic."

"Magic" prominently showcases some of Mutt Lange's distinct specialties: a huge, unforgettable three-chord guitar riff (reminiscent of the one in the "Pour Some Sugar On Me" chorus) and those memorable, super-catchy, multi-layered *"Uh-oh it's magic!"* backing vocals.

They're *so* Mutt Lange.

Huey Lewis And The News:

The familiar backing vocals in The Cars' "Magic" chorus are quite similar in arrangement to yet another '80s hit song's chorus: Huey Lewis And The News' "Do You Believe In Love" -- the band's breakout hit and first Top 10 single, which was written by...Mutt Lange.

Celine Dion:

Another song that showcases larger-than-life, glossy backing vocals is Celine Dion's "Goodbye's (The Saddest Word)," written and produced by Mutt Lange.

All you need to hear are eight seconds from the song -- starting at the 10-second mark -- to recognize Mutt Lange's unmistakable backing vocals and realize his involvement.

Billy Ocean:

Mutt Lange was behind some of Billy Ocean's biggest hit songs; he co-wrote and co-produced the '80s track "Loverboy," and -- as Mutt has a penchant for unique, long song titles -- "Get Outta My Dreams, Get Into My Car" and "When The Going Gets Tough, The Tough Get Going."

"Get Outta My Dreams, Get into My Car" also showcases yet another Mutt Lange song technique, officially referred to as octave-displacement: when a chorus's infectious sing-along harmonies haven't already been driven across enough, the song modulates to take the chorus up another key, to drive the melody even further into your brain.

Loverboy:

Loverboy's Top 10 '80s hit song "Lovin' Every Minute Of It" was written by Mutt Lange. Interestingly, even though Mutt did not produce the song, Tom Allom -- the producer of Def Leppard's debut album *On Through The Night* -- did. Leppard worlds collided!

Foreigner:

Foreigner's album *4* sold over seven million copies in the U.S. alone, was the band's first (and only) #1 album in the States, featured the hit songs "Urgent," "Juke Box Hero," and power-ballad "Waiting For A Girl Like You," and was co-produced by Mutt Lange (with Foreigner's Mick Jones). Unsurprisingly, the album also features Mutt's backing vocals.

Heart:

Heart's hit song "All I Wanna Do Is Make Love To You" and

the ultra-infectious ballad "Will You Be There (In The Morning)" were both written by Mutt Lange.

Michael Bolton:

Michael Bolton's hit song "Said I Loved You But I Lied" -- which topped *Billboard*'s Adult Contemporary chart and received gold sales certification as a single -- was co-produced and co-written by Mutt Lange.

The Corrs:

The band's internationally successful pop tune "Breathless" (their only #1 single in the U.K., and only Top 40 hit in the U.S.) was co-written and produced by Mutt Lange.

Lady Gaga:

Lady Gaga's song "You And I" -- which, prior to its release, she teased fans that "someone legendary" would be producing it -- has a country/rock flair that elicits thoughts of Shania Twain and Queen. That shouldn't be surprising though, as the song was co-produced by Mutt Lange (with Lady Gaga) and features his unmistakable backing vocals.

The "We Will Rock You" beats and claps are all the more fitting since Queen's Brian May plays electric guitar on the track.

Collaborating with Mutt Lange should have been expected, as Lady Gaga had expressed being a fan of Def Leppard's style of music:

> "With my music, there's lots of really big Def Leppard-style melodies in the choruses... I have created a genre of metal/dance/techno/rock/pop music with a lot of anthemic choruses because that is actually the music I love." -- *Lady Gaga, The Sun*

Maroon 5:

Maroon 5's pop song "Misery" was produced by Mutt Lange. It's the standout track from the album *Hands All Over*, also produced by Mutt. And while he is not listed as an official songwriter on the album, Mutt's influence on composing the songs was still prevalent, as divulged by lead singer Adam Levine in an interview with *Rolling Stone*:

> "[Mutt] worked me harder than anyone ever has. I would come in with a finished song, and he'd say, 'That's a good start. Now strip it down to the drums and start over.' The coolest thing about him is that not only has he been a huge, legendary producer, but he also is a legit, serious writer."

Britney Spears:

Britney Spears' ballad "Don't Let Me Be The Last To Know," off of her album *Oops!...I Did It Again* was produced and co-written by Mutt Lange (and then-wife Shania Twain).

Backing vocals are prominent throughout the song, courtesy of, well, who else but Mutt Lange.

Nickelback:

Nickelback's *Dark Horse* album was co-produced by Mutt Lange; he was also involved in composing multiple tracks, including the album's lead single and standout track, "Gotta Be Somebody."

Frontman Chad Kroeger spoke to Billboard.com about working with his "hero" on the album, and provided some insight on Mutt's recording process:

"[Mutt] likes those big gang vocals, those 'heys' and 'yeahs.' That was new for us. There might be six of us sitting around a microphone, just screaming the same line over and over and over for, like, 20 minutes straight, and you start stacking it up and get this huge wall that sounds like...an arena full of people. That's the way Mutt pictures everything. Mutt looks at it one way and one way only -- it's you standing on stage in front of nine million people. And when it's a love song, it's you singing to a girl in the first row. And when it's a rock song, it's gotta be you singing to every single person, with their hand pumping in the air. That's how he looks at it, and he never wavers."

He also noted how challenging it can be to perform Mutt's studio creations live in concert:

"[Mutt]'s not willing to budge when it comes to screaming higher and harder. There were a few times where I would have to say to him, 'Listen, I'm gonna have to sing this live,' and he was like, 'Yeah, but we're not gonna sacrifice this record for that sentiment.' So I really just had to suck it up. You gotta figure the guy knows what he's doing."

This comment can easily apply to Def Leppard as well. For instance, performing a song like "Photograph" and its demanding upper-register lead vocals in concert, not to mention decades after its release, or even having to reimagine and reconstruct "Love Bites" in order to perform it live.

"I remember, we'd never done 'Love Bites' [live] as a band...it was strictly a studio song. But it went to No. 1

on the Billboard charts while we were on tour in America, so it was like...'We're gonna have to learn it.' We booked a rehearsal studio in Vancouver for two days, and we were frantically learning it, like, 'What's the most prominent guitar part and how can I play that and sing it?' It was scary." -- Phil Collen, MusicRadar.com

Muse:

Mutt Lange produced Muse's Grammy-award-winning concept album *Drones*, which debuted at #1 on *Billboard*'s top albums chart.

Muse's frontman had this to say about working with Mutt Lange:

"Before I met him I wasn't sure. I didn't want us to be turned into a kind of top 40 act. I figured Mutt would be more focused on, 'What's the single? What's going to be the big hit?' He wasn't like that at all... He's the kind of person to get into the mind of the artist and whatever the artist wants... You feel like you're in the presence of some sort of guru, or spiritual outsider." -- Matt Bellamy, LouderSound.com

The album's mix engineer shared his thoughts on Mutt's recording process:

"He has a surreal concentration level and an amazing ability to recall every aspect of each take. This allows him to nail comps [taking the best parts of multiple takes and piecing them together to create one 'perfect take'] as they are done... Mutt has the best ears imaginable. [He] would go into note–by–note detail on a level *that was incredible to me. It was almost superhuman. He'll close his eyes, and then say, 'This bar is too long,' or 'That bar is rushed.'" -- Tommaso Colliva, SoundOn-Sound.com*

Superstar Record Producer ... And More

While more examples can be cited, the projects mentioned above should provide a good representation of Mutt Lange's incalculable contributions to artists' careers. Without his involvement, an argument could be made that some of those music acts' superstar trajectories definitely would have been different, if not less stellar.

That's the kind of unique game changer Mutt Lange is.

> "To be quite honest, I don't know anybody else who can do what Mutt does."
> -- Phil Collen, Guitar World

An article in *The Economist* spotlighting AC/DC's *Back In Black* album specifically made note of Mutt Lange's production, and brilliantly described his inimitable contributions this way:

> "[Mutt Lange] made the artists he worked with sound not like him, but a version of themselves they could not have been without him."

It wouldn't be hyperbole to say if an artist has worked with Mutt Lange, the song or album he was involved in is likely the most notable, successful project in their catalog.

The Magical Mysteria Of Mutt Lange

Def Leppard's phenomenal success with Mutt Lange only reinforces the exceptional collaborative chemistry showcased on *High 'n' Dry*, *Pyromania*, and *Hysteria*.

> "I think it says a lot that we did three records with him. Nobody else has done that many. Yes, you can mention AC/DC, but after Bon Scott died, they were desperate, and I'm sure he wouldn't have been their choice for 'Back In Black' otherwise."
> -- Joe Elliott, Record Collector magazine

Mutt Lange's fingerprints are all over Def Leppard's releases, not just the albums he produced for the band but every subsequent release since *Hysteria*.

> "Def Leppard would not have made it this far without giving people good music, and Mutt is a big part of that. He helped us to shape the songs and he kicked our butts to get the best performances out of us. We think of him as a sixth member of our group. Without him, I don't think we'd be where we are now." -- Joe Elliott, Rock Fever magazine

Here's what is fascinating about Joe's quote above: It's from 1984, several years *before* the release of *Hysteria*, which only affirms Mutt's immense, long-lasting impact on the band's career.

Undoubtedly, Mutt Lange helped Def Leppard find their sound and was crucial in helping them become the band they always dreamed of.

> *"We set out to be the biggest band in the world. And for a short while, we were."*
> -- Joe Elliott, Classic Rock magazine

Even though the band's days as a radio staple and an album sales juggernaut are in the rearview mirror, the legend of Mutt Lange lives on; he is the architect who helped create a sound platform for Def Leppard to stand on, thrive, and continue to evolve.

> *"Mutt Lange is everything to us. He made us seem special. Without him, we'd have just been another ordinary rock band. He's always the most talented person in the room, and can play anything or sing everything we do, only better. He's so inspiring that you want to do your absolute best just to please him... He certainly helped us to develop the style and sound Leppard are known for."*
> -- Phil Collen, Record Collector magazine

The Elephant In The Room

No doubt there are some music enthusiasts, including a faction of Def Leppard fans, who are not admirers of Mutt Lange's work, convinced that the projects he's been involved in are too overproduced, and in the case of Def Leppard, too commercial and pop-lite.

In addition, some feel Mutt Lange *derailed* Def Leppard's career with *Pyromania* and *Hysteria* -- chart performance be damned! -- believing the band's first two albums were their best and each subsequent album underwhelmed, to put it mildly. Put simply, Def Leppard, a band whose roots once had a more raw and harder edge, sold out and became "soft" because of Mutt.

> "Whatever you want to call us, it's water off a duck's back, because Def Leppard has only improved musically, vocally and production-wise over the four albums we've done. They've been similar in their aspect of music -- they've always been commercially-oriented. I don't care what people say, we haven't sold out, we've always been that way, and we will continue to be that way.
> -- Joe Elliott, Metal Muscle magazine (1989)

To each their own, but it bears repeating that it was Mutt Lange who produced Def Leppard's prestigious second album, *High 'n' Dry*. And it was *On Through The Night* that captured his interest and attention in the first place, as he recognized Def Leppard's potential and wanted to help the band further utilize its budding talents.

Conceivably, Def Leppard's career would have been cut far short had Mutt Lange not gotten involved in guiding the band during its formative years and beyond. That said, a career spanning over four decades and filled with a multitude of unforgettable hit songs is far better than being a one-hit-wonder. Safe to say, solely relying on, say, *On Through The Night* to define "the best of" Def Leppard would be incredibly limiting and short-sighted.

> "When 'Hysteria' first came out, a lot of people went, 'Dude, this is lame. This isn't rock. It's pop. It's wussy.' But actually, it had the absolute effect it was supposed to have had. Because the point was to not just play to the rock audience but rather to play to everybody. And we achieved that."
> -- Phil Collen, Guitar World

As for Def Leppard's sound going "soft" due to Mutt, as if he debilitates rock bands he works with, AC/DC's Mutt-produced albums *Highway to Hell*, *Back In Black*, and *For Those About to Rock We Salute You* would beg to differ. What's more, those three AC/DC albums are unquestionably AC/DC, just like *High 'n' Dry*, *Pyromania*, and *Hysteria* undeniably exhibit a multifaceted Def Leppard.

> "I hear a lot of people say, 'High 'n' Dry is my favorite Def Leppard album.' And it's like, yeah, but that sound was kind of borrowed from AC/DC, which in some ways was a Mutt thing as well. It very much had that vibe. To me, Def Leppard didn't start to sound unique until Pyromania, which crossed over, and then Hysteria, which really crossed over."
> -- Phil Collen, Guitar World

The Legend Of Mutt Lange

Mutt Lange's extremely private, publicity-shy persona only adds to his mystique and uber-producer status. Clearly, he prefers to let the music do the talking for him -- figuratively and literally -- as he remains behind the scenes, letting others enjoy the fame and accolades.

With all the immense success he's achieved over the decades, he's certainly earned that right and is free to go about things however he wants.

It's only fitting that at Def Leppard's 2019 Rock and Roll Hall of Fame induction ceremony, the band (courtesy of Joe Elliott's acceptance speech) made sure to recognize their "mentor" Mutt Lange -- who, shockingly, is *not* in the Rock and Roll Hall of Fame -- noting how important he was to their career:

"*The most significant contribution that [previous band managers] Peter [Mensch] and Cliff [Burnstein] ever made...was introducing our music to our future producer, co-writer and mentor, Mr. Robert John "Mutt" Lange. We first worked with Mutt in 1981 on an album called 'High & Dry,' but it was 1983 that saw us move into a whole new orbit with the phenomenal success of the album 'Pyromania'...*"

And as the renowned story goes, *Hysteria* followed and the rest is history.

By the way, did you happen to catch the look of pride on Mutt Lange's face in the audience as Joe Elliott spoke those heartfelt words of appreciation?

Never mind. He wasn't in attendance.

That's *so* Mutt Lange.

Personal Story: Poor Sav...And Go, Joe!

Def Leppard sometimes participated in promotional soccer events, typically as part of a local radio station's promotion, where station personnel and contest winners would play on teams with and against members of the band.

On this particular '90s day, Joe, Sav, Viv, and Malvin (the band's tour manager) participated in the exhibition, arriving soon before game time in a non-descript shuttle that transported them from their hotel.

I was given the option to take part in the game but instead chose to be an observer from the sidelines, watching the action from the designated Def Leppard team bench area.

Once on the field, Joe's competitive spirit was on full display, as he put his "game face" on and hair up in a ponytail. Vivian (behind him) followed suit...

Once all the players got into position at the center of the field, it was go-time. Let the game begin!

Joe's strategy of residing by the opposing team's goal area would work out splendidly, as he was usually unguarded...

Not very long into the start of the game -- *POW!* -- Sav was involved in a collision of knees, the result of several players simultaneously and aggressively going after the soccer ball.

Sav let out a distinct yelp at the moment of impact, followed by him immediately falling to the ground. Not only did his exclamation of pain sound concerning, but what was just as worrisome was the difficulty he had getting back on his feet or even putting some weight on his stricken leg.

A few of us headed over to help Sav up and sturdy him, helping take his body weight off his impacted knee so he could slowly limp over to the sidelines.

An ice pack was provided to him to apply to his knee, which he did while hunched over in a chair, clearly in discomfort...

Meanwhile, the action on the soccer field continued. Joe seemed to reawaken his Pelé-like soccer skills and kicked them into high gear -- literally -- as he repeatedly scored while being cheered on by the crowd.

Even after falling over at one point while chasing the ball, Joe was still able to kick it into the goal from the ground...

GOAL!

Go, Joe!

Whether kicking the ball from the ground or in mid-air, Joe showcased his soccer skills...

ANOTHER GOAL!

Go, Joe!

Some fans in the stands lost count of how many goals he had

scored, yelling out and asking him what his tally was. Joe obliged and provided an update, holding up four fingers...

Here is Vivian congratulating Joe's impressive performance...

With all the action happening on the field, I don't think Joe realized Sav had been hurt. He had been so focused on the game and getting quite a workout in the process...

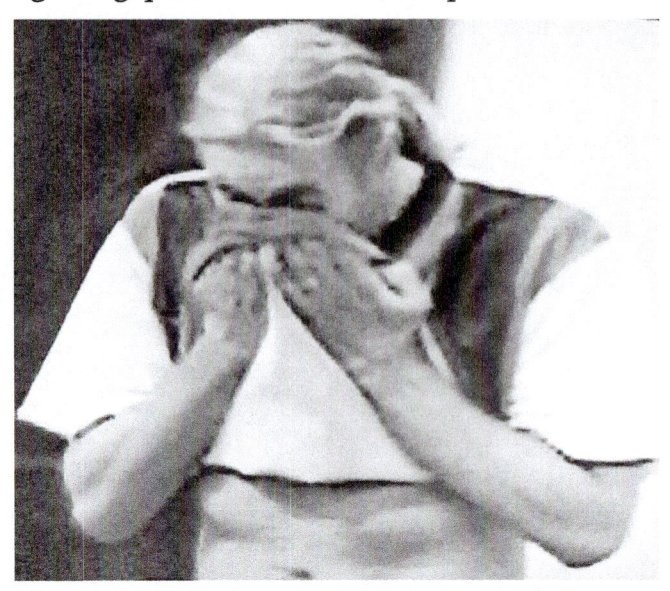

It wasn't until a game break that Joe finally had a chance to catch his breath and grab some water, and also get a look at an ailing Sav on the sidelines...

Joe walked over to check on him and see how he was feeling...

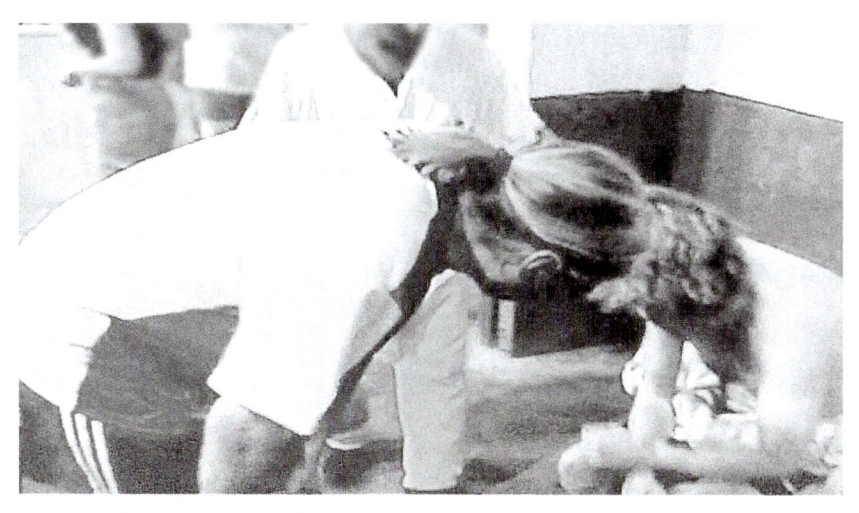

Soon after, a medical professional in the stands came over to the area to offer his help. He felt around Sav's kneecap, applying a bit of pressure to better evaluate the injury's location and how serious it might be...

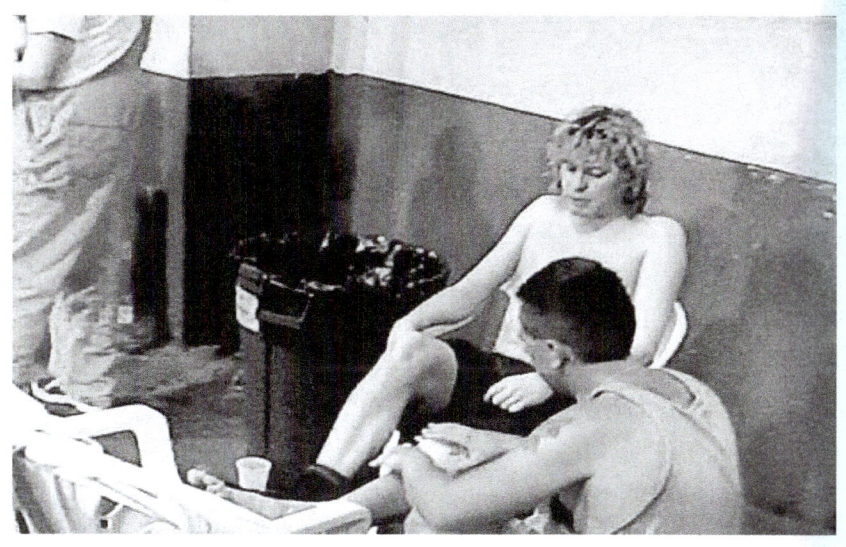

Luckily, he determined the kneecap (and the area surrounding it) felt alright and didn't find anything very concerning, but said there would be some soreness and a potential bruise. For the time being, Sav's knee was wrapped up for support...

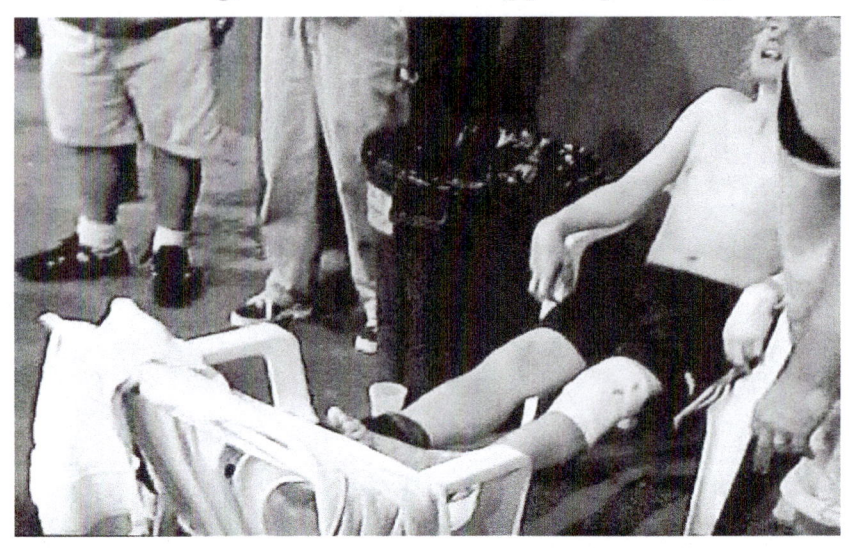

Fortunately, after some time, Sav's knee pain subsided enough that he was able to put weight back on his leg and start walking around on his own, watching the game and cheering on his team from the bench...

After the game was over, the guys took the time to sign autographs for fans in the stands who came out to watch them play. Sav felt well enough to take part too, sans his left shoe and sock...

Later that day, Sav confirmed his knee was feeling better -- as witnessed by his flawless performance during the band's concert that evening, not to mention partaking in the pre-show fan meet and greet. (It would have been so unfortunate if Sav had been seriously hurt during the game, making this event memorable for all the wrong reasons!)

On a broader note, oh how I wish smartphones existed during these days, to easily and conveniently capture moments like this soccer game. Being the '90s, a clunky 8mm camcorder would sometimes have to suffice, and it did just that in this instance -- the soccer game photos in this chapter are actually screen grabs from my video archive.

Thankfully, the video footage from this event remains part of my prized collection of special Def Leppard memories!

Personal Story: And Now A Quick Break For The Scent Of Glitter

This backstage sticker pass is from the "Soccer Rocks The Globe" kick-off concert event which occurred in June 1994 at Chicago's UIC Pavilion.

WORLD CUP '94 KICK OFF
SOCCER ROCKS THE GLOBE
6/16/94

BACKSTAGE

I didn't know much about the event itself back then, except that a CD compilation was being released that included music acts (from various record labels) who were partaking in the event. All I knew was some of the artists featured on the CD would be performing at the concert.

I attended the event to show my support for the CD, which we were releasing and promoting. Other than that, there really wasn't much else to do, as this wasn't a "work" event.

While chatting with several coworkers from the label at the venue before the start of the show, someone mentioned to me that members of Def Leppard, or at least Joe, were in attendance at the backstage area, just to watch the festivities. I thought they were joking; they were well aware of my affinity for the band, and could have been trying to get a reaction out of me. (It had happened before! Always in a good-natured way, of course.)

Joke or not, I made the most of the pass I had and took a walk, making my way to the backstage area.

The central "backstage" consisted of a long plain hallway with solid, nondescript doors, seemingly for the various artists who were there to perform. That being said, it wasn't clear who was located in a room or whether it was even in use.

Not only did it look and feel odd, I felt out of place. This wasn't a typical backstage, at least one I was used to, especially since there wasn't a main touring act, where everyone backstage was focusing on the same objective.

This was a mish-mash of sorts.

Continuing with my walk, it was intriguing to come across some of the frenzied scenes surrounding the backstage area, most notably people scurrying around, and making sure the multi-artist event was going off without a hitch.

I ended up deciding to pick a backstage spot where I could simply stay out of everyone's way while taking it all in. I chose to stand up against a wall in the aforementioned long plain hallway, with its series of room doors still closed.

And that's when one of the most surreal experiences I've ever encountered occurred.

All of a sudden, I heard what could be best described as a "ruckus" that was increasingly getting louder. Specifically, the noise consisted of numerous male voices coming from one of the rooms.

Another way to describe it was that it sounded like overhearing a sports team in their locker room being riled by their coach's motivational speech, getting worked up into a frenzy to get their "game face" on and game-day attitudes in check.

And hearing all this while the room's door was still closed -- at several points, the yells sounded like there was an argument among them -- it was definitely loud.

Baffled by it all, I wondered what the heck was going on. And was there a security team on staff nearby if needed?

Just then, the door to the room burst open and a bunch of guys in silver trench coats marched out, surrounding the center of their attention: Gary Glitter, bare-chested in a bright silvery sleeveless leather outfit with matching wrist/forearm cuffs, and his hair extraordinarily poofed up and sprayed to the extreme to stay in place.

The group made their way down the hallway toward me. All I could do was be mesmerized by the spectacle, just idly standing there, watching them march by.

If you would like to go beyond simply envisioning this, I recommend searching the web for Gary Glitter and Soccer Rocks the Globe. It will show you the otherworldly outfits and appearances I'm referring to. And if you can find it, just imagine standing in an empty corridor with this group of people marching by you.

Gary Glitter's entourage practically encircled him as they made their way to the stage area for their performance. With every step Gary took, his group chanted and cheered him on. And he fed off of their over-the-top rally cries, pushing up each of his leather jacket sleeves while walking, like someone about to rumble. He was literally the "leader of the gang," just like the name of one of his songs.

This all must have been part of his pre-show warm-up routine.

Now, mind you, I was backstage looking to see if anyone from Def Leppard was in attendance, and chose what I thought was a spot out of peoples' way. Never did I expect to witness something so bizarre. I didn't even know Gary Glitter was performing at this event! It was unexpected to say the least, especially being such a huge glam rock fan -- a perplexed, bewildered one but glam rock fan nonetheless!

After the mini-parade of Gary Glitter and his posse marched right by me, acting like they were leading him to a prizefight he'd be participating in, I'd say within about 3 seconds I was overwhelmed by the most powerful scent of perfume. The fragrance emanating from the group lingered in the air long after Gary and his group (aka chanters) made their way down the length of the hallway.

By the way, in case you weren't aware, Glitter's most popular song is "Rock and Roll Part 2" (best known as the "Hey" song played in sports venues). You'll likely hear some similarities between the song and Def Leppard's tracks "Back In Your Face" and "C'mon, C'mon."

Back to my original story... I honestly don't recall ever seeing any member of Def Leppard in the backstage area or at the concert, but I will never forget the everlasting, pungent smell of perfume from that day.

All that glitters most definitely isn't always gold.

Personal Story: The Ballad Of Joe (Reflections & An Appreciation)

I felt compelled to dedicate a chapter to Joe Elliott, to recognize and celebrate some of his accomplishments, which are all the more impressive when further dissected, and to also reflect on and share some of my fondest interactions with him that I felt his fans would enjoy reading about.

First, I have to say that one thought that has repeatedly popped into my head while delving into some of the memories for this book is that I was in my early-to-mid twenties when these events occurred. (To put that further into perspective, Joe was in his mid-30s.) Hence, the realization: I'm now about twice the age I was from back then, and, as of this writing, Joe is in his early sixties! Where has the time gone!?

Anyway... *Do you really, really wanna do this now*? Ok... *Let's go*!

In my opinion, there's a particular song that fittingly describes Joe and his journey to rock stardom. And, ironically, it's *not* a Def Leppard song.

The song I'm referring to is..."Irene Wilde."

Assuming that some readers haven't heard of this song before, here's some context: it was released in 1976, written and performed by Ian Hunter. Ian was the lead singer of the tragically underrated glam band Mott The Hoople, a favorite of Joe's, whose classic '70s anthem "All The Young Dudes" is considered Joe's all-time favorite song.

Ian Hunter departed Mott The Hoople and went on to enjoy a successful solo career which included hit songs like "Once Bitten, Twice Shy" (yes, the same song Great White remade in 1989) and "Cleveland Rocks" (a remake of that song was used for the opening credit sequence of "The Drew Carey Show"). Do you recall Barry Manilow's 1979 hit song "Ships"? That, too, was a remake of an Ian Hunter song. (There are *so many* more Ian Hunter songs that deserve just as much attention, but I'll leave it at that.)

Ian Hunter was one of Joe's music idols growing up, back when he aspired to be a "rock star," even daydreaming about it during his day job at a Sheffield spoon factory.

In 1976, Ian released his solo album *All-American Alien Boy*, which included a vast array of enjoyable song offerings, but there was one specific track -- a piano ballad -- that, to this day, stands out as a fan favorite, especially when performed live: "Irene Wilde"

Ian's lyrics for the song are autobiographical. Irene Wilde is the name of a girl from his youth, the object of his unrequited love, and even though her name is reflected in the song's title, it's *really* all about Ian and his own personal journey.

More specifically, Irene Wilde rejected Ian (at his hometown's bus station) at the age of sixteen. This is all beautifully told in the song's heartfelt opening lyrics: *"When I was just sixteen, I stood waiting for a dream, at Barker street bus station every night..."*

But there is a deeper, underlying meaning to the song's supposed message about rejection: it's about overcoming, embracing a challenge, and using it as a motivational quest to achieve whatever goal you set out to accomplish.

In Ian's case, it's what drove him to want to be the music artist he would ultimately become *("In my mother's living room, I composed so many tunes...")* and keeping the faith that he would never let up until he reached his dream, as noted in what would be the song's most poignant lyrics: *"I'm gonna be somebody, some day."*

Now let's circle back to Joe, who in 1975 was already envisioning his imaginary band "Deaf Leopard" selling out venues with its imaginary concerts. I can't help but think that 16-year-old Joe -- the same age Ian Hunter harkens back to in "Irene Wilde" -- repeatedly listened to that song in January 1976 (the year of the album's release) and felt the same motivation and passion, singing right along with his music idol, *"I'm gonna be somebody, some day."*

I'm sure it struck a chord with Joe, no pun intended.

By 1977, Joe's vision already began to take shape: he had hooked up with Pete Willis and Rick Savage. And by 1978, his "Deaf Leopard" band idea would morph into "Def Leppard," Steve Clark would join the band, and the rest is history. Within five years, the band would be headlining their *Pyromania* tour. *I'm gonna be somebody, some day* -- goodbye spoon factory!

"Irene Wilde" is about triumphing over seemingly insurmountable odds, never giving up, and making a dream come true. Joe's success with Def Leppard is *his* "Irene Wilde," further bolstered by the fact that the song originated from one of his music heroes.

Not only did Joe achieve his dream, he went on to befriend the music idols who provided him with that motivation: Ian Hunter was no longer just a favorite artist he'd listen to on a vinyl record or radio station but a friend and mentor; Joe would go on to perform his beloved "All The Young Dudes" *with* Ian Hunter countless times in concert.

The same can be said of Queen, another band that had a huge influence on Joe (and the rest of Def Leppard). What a gratifying achievement to go from simply being a major Queen superfan to actually becoming dear friends (see what I did there?), as it was Queen's legendary guitarist Brian May that Def Leppard chose to induct them into the Rock and Roll Hall of Fame. (Brian graciously did just that with a heartfelt, eloquent speech.)

I'm reminded of an unforgettable conversation I had with Joe back in the mid-'90s during the *Slang* tour when we discussed a topic we both loved: glam music. The song I brought up which led off the glam discussion was Def Leppard's remake of "Action." (The original version appeared on Sweet's album *Desolation Boulevard*, which also included "Ballroom Blitz," one of their biggest hits.)

Def Leppard's "Action" was included on *Retro Active*, which had been released a few years prior to this particular discussion with Joe. My initial comment to him was about what a superb job the band did in remaking Sweet's classic -- on *Retro Active* as well as live in concert -- transforming it into an even more power-driven, melodic rocker.

This segued into me asking Joe my next question, something I genuinely wondered, yet admittedly asked only half-jokingly and out of my own selfish interest, being a glam rock fan of acts like Mott the Hoople, Ian Hunter, Queen, T-Rex, Sweet, David Bowie's Ziggy Stardust, Slade, Mick Ronson, and so on.

I asked Joe: "Why don't you guys record more glam remakes, like a Mott The Hoople song?" Joe's eyes lit up and he smiled, then responded with a laugh, "They won't let me!" He was jokingly referring to the rest of the band, motioning to some of the other band members who were scattered around the hotel suite-turned-bar room we were in, then adding that he'd *love* to perform more -- a lot more -- of the glam classics he grew up with if it were only up to him.

What was so memorable to me about this discussion was that, at least for a brief moment, it no longer felt like I was having a conversation with Def Leppard's lead singer; instead, it seemed like I was talking to the kid from Sheffield who aspired to follow in the footsteps of the music idols he so endeared, discussing a subject that brought him absolute joy.

I found it so interesting looking back at this conversation in subsequent years (and decades), thinking about how gratifying -- and frankly, inevitable -- it must have been for Joe to begin working on side projects like the David Bowie tribute band Cybernauts (which also included Phil Collen), and, ultimately, his passion project Down 'n' Outz, initially a Mott The Hoople tribute band that would end up also releasing original glam-influenced music material of their own.

In hindsight, Joe's deeper involvement in the glam rock universe makes a lot of sense, as the seeds for these types of projects were planted long ago: *Retro Active* not only included Sweet's "Action" (which had already been released as a B-side on Def Leppard's "Make Love Like A Man" single), but also Mick Ronson's "Only After Dark" (originally a B-side on the "Let's Get Rocked" single).

Retro Active also included an updated version of Def Leppard's vintage track "Ride Into The Sun," this time with a brand new, rockin', honky-tonk piano introduction performed by none other than Joe's music-hero-turned-close-friend, Ian Hunter.

Years later, not only did Def Leppard release *Yeah!* in 2006, a covers album showcasing each band member's musical influences from the '60s and '70s, but Joe's Down 'n' Outz band (solely a tribute band at the time) ended up being the opening act for the Ian Hunter-led Mott The Hoople reunion tour in

2009.

It's not surprising that Down 'n' Outz's third album, *This Is How We Roll*, featured original material. Some may consider it serendipity, but I wholeheartedly believe the project was decades in the making, with Joe's long-brewing aspirations *finally* coming to fruition.

As silly as it may sound, my reaction when listening to the album for the very first time was a lot of...smiling. That's it, just smiling. I know that doesn't qualify as much of a critique but it took me right back to my glam music discussion with him from the '90s. Roughly thirty years later, *This Is How We Roll* was the byproduct of Joe's ceaseless glam ambitions being taken further -- much further -- and far beyond simply recording more covers.

The new music brought to mind a kid living it up in a glam rock candy store whose aisles overflowed with varieties of David Bowie, Mott The Hoople, Ian Hunter, and numerous other artists, with songs that not only showcased Joe's childhood music influences but also included hints of Def Leppard sprinkled throughout -- how could they not?

Here is a quick sampling of the little nuances I heard after a couple of listens:

> **"Walk to Babylon"** -- The song's melody echoes the *"You're all that I want..."* chorus from Def Leppard's "We Belong," which Joe penned. Reportedly, "We Belong" was initially conceived by Joe as a Mott The Hoople-like "All The Young Dudes" anthem, so the correlation isn't all that surprising.
>
> **"Boys Don't Cry"** -- At the song's 2:30 mark, Def Leppard's *"All we want to hear is the audience applause"* lyric (and portion) from the song "On Through The Night" (off of the *High 'n' Dry*

album) comes to mind.

- **"Creatures"** -- The spoken lyric "*These human games*" at the 2:47 mark took me immediately back to Mott The Hoople's track "Saturday Gigs," which features Ian Hunter speaking the classic lyric, "*A grown-up game*" right before the song builds to its crescendo.

- **"Let It Shine"** -- The prominent keyboards evoke Mott The Hoople's keyboardists (Verden Allen as well as Morgan Fisher), whose contributions made for some of Mott's most unforgettable piano-driven songs, one example being "Through The Looking Glass."

- **"Music Box"** -- Stirs up thoughts of Ian Hunter's lovely little gem titled "The Ballad of Little Star."

- **"White Punks On Dope"** -- While this track is a cover of a song originally recorded by The Tubes, Down 'n' Outz's version features Ian Hunter-esque piano playing which conjures up memories of Mott The Hoople's classic song "The Golden Age of Rock 'n' Roll" as well as "All The Way From Memphis" (which incidentally is the medley Ian himself played at the beginning of *Retro Active*'s updated version of Def Leppard's "Ride Into The Sun.")

These are just *some* examples.

I encourage you to listen to those Down 'n' Outz songs, as well as revisit the older songs referenced, and see if you agree!

Music attributions similar to the ones mentioned also sneak into Def Leppard's songs periodically. Some examples: The chorus for "Demolition Man" brings to mind Sweet's "Ballroom Blitz" chorus; "Back In Your Face" and its '*heys*' emulate the predominant *Hey!* repeated throughout Gary Glitter's "Rock and

Roll Part 2" (aka "The Hey Song"); the "We Belong" lyric "*If you cast the first stone, I will roll it away*" is no doubt a wonderful wink and tip of the hat to Mott The Hoople's song "Roll Away The Stone"; Def Leppard's "Nine Lives" lyric "*I've been bitten once, but I won't be twice shy*" is a quaint reference to Ian Hunter's song "Once Bitten Twice Shy"; the arrangement of Def Leppard's ballad "Love" undoubtedly echoes Queen's song "Jealousy." And so on.

By the way, the title of this chapter is itself an ode to the classic Mott the Hoople song "The Ballad of Mott," which seemed quite fitting considering the subject matter. Joe's music roots remain proudly on display to this day; in case you weren't aware, his well-known "*Don't forget us, we won't forget you*" farewell line at Def Leppard's shows originated with Ian Hunter, who would say the phrase at the end of Mott The Hoople's shows.

During the times I had the opportunity to have a chat with Joe, one of my first (and favorite) questions I'd ask him was, "How's Ian Hunter doing?" It was easily a discussion topic we both enjoyed. Ironically, years later, in the early 2000s, I finally had the opportunity to meet Ian Hunter myself by attending a backstage party after one of his solo shows. More importantly, I was able to (nervously) tell Ian how much I admired his work going back to the Mott The Hoople days. Unforgettably, Ian, being ever so humble, responded that he was just really glad to meet a passionate fan who didn't have any gray hair on their head.

After chatting with him for a couple of minutes, I made it a point to tell him, "Whenever I've had the opportunity to talk to Joe Elliott in the past, I would always ask him how you were doing, so I just wanted to ask you...How's Joe doing?" Ian indulged my request and went on to provide me with an update on his friend, adding that he had just spoken to Joe on the phone a couple of weeks prior. It was nice to hear the update

-- besides the fact that it was being provided by Ian freakin' Hunter! -- since at the time Def Leppard had been away from the public eye for quite a while, working on what would be their *X* album. Simply having the opportunity to have a one-on-one discussion with Ian was wonderful, unforgettable, and *very* surreal.

Joe was kind enough to recommend a CD to me during a chat on another occasion. The topic of Mott The Hoople came up (big surprise, right?), and Joe brought to my attention a *very* unique compilation I hadn't heard of before which was about to be released in the U.S., explaining to me that it featured Japanese bands performing Mott The Hoople songs.

I ended up getting the CD, titled *Moth Poet Hotel*. At times, I'd listen to it in my car while driving around with friends, and they'd be *very* quick to ask what the heck I was listening to. (It's a unique release, and *exactly* how Joe had described it to me.) After answering their question about what I was "forcing" them to listen to, they would inevitably follow-up with something along the lines of, "Where did you even hear about this?," and I'd tell them: "Joe Elliott." Soon after, another question: "Where? In an interview?," wondering where (and why) Joe would have spoken about such an odd release. It was always amusing to respond, "No, Joe Elliott literally told me about this CD and to check it out."

It was gratifying being a passionate Def Leppard fan not long out of college to be able to say something like that.

And I still have the CD to this day. Do I still listen to it? Nope, but it still makes for a great memory!

While working at the band's record label, and back when compact discs were the latest and greatest music products, I had put in a product order request through the record company to get KISS's entire remastered catalog on CD for Joe. (KISS was on the same record label as Def Leppard.) I figured the remastered CD collection would be something he'd enjoy, not only because he was such an avid music collector (you can see part of his expansive collection in the "Miss You In A Heartbeat" video), but more so as something to listen to while continuously being out on the road. (On a related note, I had a friend who worked at a film studio back when VHS videocassettes were still popular, so I was able to collect a box of VHS movies for Vivian, who I had promised I'd get for him and the band, so they could have a collection of films to watch to help pass the time on bus rides between tour stops.)

Def Leppard's tour was returning to the Midwest (which is where I was located at the time) for a few dates, so I was able to give Joe the box containing the 25 or so remastered KISS CDs backstage before one of their shows. Malvin Mortimer, Def Leppard's tour manager at the time, happened to walk by at precisely the moment I was handing the CD-filled box over to Joe and purposefully tried to intercept the exchange, joking "Oh, is that for me?" Without hesitation or missing a beat in our discussion, Joe immediately responded back to Malvin, "Fook off!" (phonetic spelling, of course). It was a lighthearted moment, and also emblematic of the rapport Malvin had with the band during that period.

Malvin's interjection aside, Joe was very appreciative when I explained what the box contained, responding with an excited "Oh wow, thank you!" which genuinely came across as the sincere reaction of a passionate KISS fanatic. The memory is all the more nostalgic for me because, as you may recall, Def Leppard ended up co-headlining a tour with KISS nearly two decades after this occurrence. Surely, yet another ambitious achievement for that kid from Sheffield -- this time, touring alongside the iconic music act he grew up listening to.

"Irene Wilde" reemerges: *I'm gonna be somebody, some day.*

If you haven't already seen it, you likely can find a video clip online of Joe introducing KISS during one of Def Leppard's co-headlining tour dates, screaming KISS's famous *"You wanted the best..."* line at the top of his lungs into a microphone from the backstage area to the concert audience. Take a moment to watch Joe's reactions at that moment -- before, during, and after his announcement. It's a terrific instance that perfectly captures some of the glimpses I've made references to, specifically of that passionate, music-loving kid that's always residing within.

It's another reminder that no matter how aspirational some dreams seem, they *do* come true and Joe Elliott is a prime example. The childhood ambition of one day rising to superstardom in a rock band that would sell out venues across the globe may have appeared far-fetched at the time, but it was achieved (and then some), as Joe would go on to become the lead singer of one of the biggest bands of the 1980s.

Decades after Def Leppard's formation, the band's popularity and success have endured -- just like the band itself -- culminating with the group's induction into the Rock & Roll Hall of Fame. And who was the special guest that performed with Def Leppard (and Queen's Brian May) during the induction ceremony's concert finale? Ian Hunter.

Joe's "Irene Wilde" journey befittingly came full circle.

Def Leppard's song "Where Does Love Go When It Dies" includes the following contemplative lyric: *If you came across your dream, would you walk on by?*

In Joe Elliott's case (and hopefully yours as well), most certainly not!

Mission definitely accomplished, Joe.

P.S.

I thought I would share at least one picture from my collection featuring yours truly and Joe backstage before one of Def Leppard's shows from back then. Here you go...

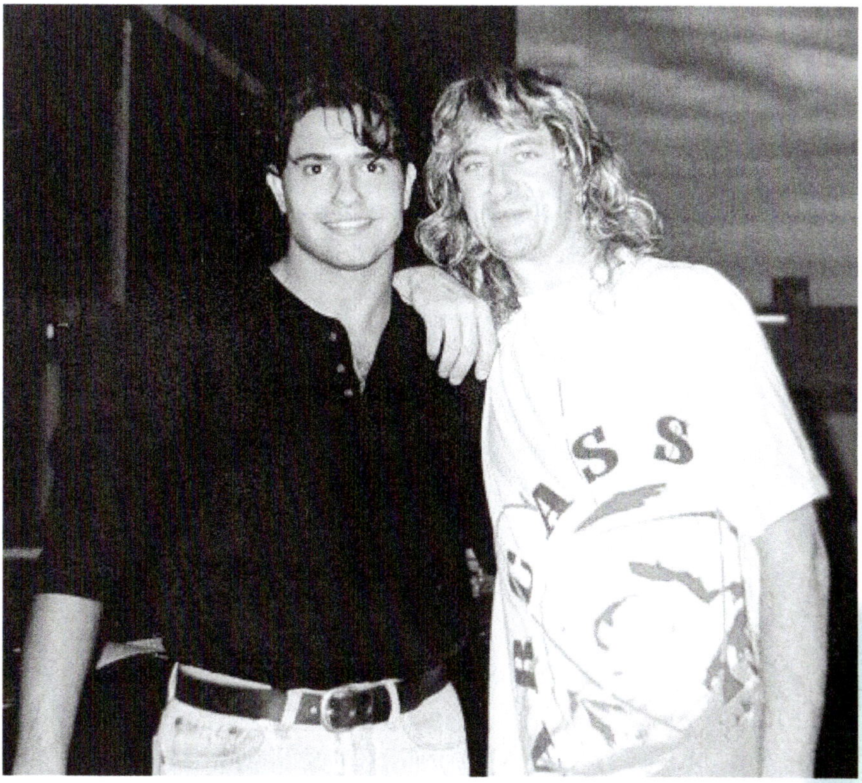

Personal Story: Meet. Greet. Repeat.

Many years ago, a "meet and greet" event typically included contest winners, radio station personnel, and representatives from music accounts (e.g., employees from record stores as well as distributors, who would supply the music product to stores), among others.

What they all had in common was they were usually big fans of the band (in this case, Def Leppard), not only there to see them in concert, but also interested in meeting them beforehand.

We would gather these guests in a room or a designated area outdoors (depending on the venue), to hang out and wait for the meet and greet to begin. (Sharing Def Leppard stories amongst themselves while they waited was the norm.)

Then all of a sudden...Oh, hello!

Members of Def Leppard would nonchalantly walk in and begin greeting people, to the attendees' wonderment and delight. Sometimes, select members would participate; other times, the entire band would attend.

(Rick, Phil, and Viv signing autographs.)

If everything went as planned, it was laid back and quite casual. Filled with anticipation, guests would patiently wait their turn as band members would make their way around the meet and greet group, making sure to "meet" and "greet" everyone in attendance.

Some interactions would take longer than others, especially when band members would be introduced to "key" attendees. For instance, employees from major music stores or influential, top-tier local radio stations -- aka sales channels that were pivotal in supporting Def Leppard. It was important to make sure the band was not only aware of the vital role these promotional outlets played but to also have the opportunity to thank them personally for it.

Oftentimes, a large, long table would be set up so items attendees brought to have autographed could be placed on and spread across. That way, each band member could have a turn signing all the materials quickly and all at once -- think of it as a production line -- thus leaving more time for them to chat with those in attendance.

I would sometimes include an item from my own collection to get signed, usually going with something more unconventional, be it a rare Def Leppard release from another country or something that wasn't even technically band-related. For example, the CD single release for the song "Don't Look Down," a track that Joe Elliott sang lead vocals on for Mick Ronson's final solo album:

There were times I noticed Joe scanning the table of items awaiting his autograph upon entering a meet and greet area, just out of his own curiosity and to get the lay of the land.

I knew if I heard an audible "Ooh" from him after seeing an item I had placed there, I had succeeded in choosing a worthy artifact. (It was an amusing challenge I put upon myself; I'm proud to report I received the hoped-for reaction on a couple of occasions.)

These types of events, which unquestionably are no longer the norm for various reasons, were considered a success if all the guests attending had their chance to meet the band, took the pictures they wanted, got their items signed, and simply had a good time.

Observing fans have the opportunity to meet their favorite band was *always* enjoyable. While repeatedly going through the motions of a meet and greet scenario could easily become monotonous -- i.e., same event, just a different town with different faces -- I never thought of it that way.

It was a blast meeting passionate fans, hearing *their* stories and sensing *their* excitement, and especially seeing their reaction when they finally got to meet the band, a moment they'd never forget.

Make no mistake, between meet and greets, bands like Def Leppard had numerous other tasks on their schedule to tend to throughout the day, including phone interviews (aka "phoners") with local radio stations or publications, making appearances at other pre-planned promotional events, going to rehearsal before the show, eating some food (can't forget that!), and also finding *some* limited personal time.

Those pressures were never on display or noticeable during Def Leppard's meet and greets, at least to me. Back then, meet and greets undoubtedly "came with the territory," but it was never a given that a band would participate, at least willingly.

Frankly, from my experiences, some music acts perceived and handled meet and greet events in a negative light. Def Leppard never fell into the category of treating them as an imposition or doing them begrudgingly.

And it goes beyond that. I hadn't realized it, at *least at first,* but Rick Allen would have low-key meet and greets of his own before the start of the "main" meet and greet event, dedicating his extra personal time to first meet people -- adults and kids -- with disabilities. It took place in a separate private area or room and out of the public eye, i.e., no fanfare or interest in having press around to publicize it. He did it because he wanted to.

For me personally, the quieter moments -- after the meet and greets were over and all the attendees had dispersed -- remain most fresh in my mind. For example, Phil Collen taking the time to discuss the benefits of being a vegetarian with me and my sister (who I had brought as my guest to one of the events, and who was contemplating becoming a vegetarian at the time). My how far Phil has come since then, not only going beyond vegetarianism with his vegan lifestyle but also incorporating intense weight training and martial arts into his routine. He's so much more physically fit now in his sixties than he was over twenty-five years ago!

*(One more photo of yours truly backstage,
this time with Rick and Phil.)*

Vivian, truly "the new guy" in the mid-'90s, was kind enough to ask me to have a seat at a table he and his then-wife were sitting at in a backstage dining area, simply to chat, knowing that I was a big Def Leppard fan. Like Phil, he didn't have to do that, but he graciously did.

To make a broader point: What were you doing back in the mid-'90s? How about now? Has a lot changed? I'm guessing it has. It just helps to put things into perspective, realizing that what Def Leppard was doing back then is *still* more or less what they are doing now: performing for and entertaining fans. That consistency and dedication are a major part of the band's appeal and longevity. Hence, while your life may have changed drastically since the days of "Photograph" and "Pour Some Sugar On Me," you can always revisit and enjoy the constant that is Def Leppard.

The same goes for meet and greets. I won't even attempt to estimate the myriad of meet and greets the band has participated in over its career, but I do know from the ones I was involved in and witnessed from back then, that they treated every person they met with newfound interest and authenticity, leaving those fans with unforgettable memories.

Thereafter, the band would move on to another tour stop in another town at another venue and do it all over again. And again. And again. And as groups of fans at those locations would await the opportunity to meet (and greet) the band, too, so they can have *their* special moments, the band would oblige, treating it just like it was the first time.

Ranking & Reviewing Def Leppard's Songs

When I first launched DefLeppardReport.com, I decided to kick things off with a mental exercise: ranking and reviewing the songs from each of the band's original studio albums.

Undoubtedly, you will disagree with some -- even many -- of the results, be it the ranking or the rationale. Nevertheless, there's a lot of good Def Leppard music to revisit!

What follows is a refreshed write-up of what was originally posted (the rankings have remained the same, the reviews have been updated). Read it at your leisure or use it as a reference guide if you like. Enjoy!

◆ ◆ ◆

Rise up and gather round for a ranking and review of all **115** songs from Def Leppard's original studio albums!

As objective as I've tried to be in providing an *honest* critique of each song, it's still just a matter of opinion. Personally, I believe even the lowest-ranked Def Leppard songs are likely still more enjoyable than most music heard on the radio these days.

This particular song ranking is specific to the band's ten original studio albums, meaning it doesn't include albums like *Yeah!* (cover songs) and *Retro Active* (B-sides compilation, etc.).

Also, I know some fans passionately believe that the *best* Def

Leppard songs are the ones from the band's early years, while others favor the music (and sound) from the late '80s and beyond. To each their own! Def Leppard's best songs aren't necessarily from one particular era or album; there's plenty to go around! That also doesn't mean that the band's most popular songs are their best ones, or vice versa.

The focus here is on ranking and assessing the songs within each of their ten studio albums (up through the self-titled *Def Leppard* release), not to critique which era of the band or album was better than the other.

Hope you find this endeavor to be entertaining.

Album: *On Through The Night*

#11 "Satellite"

The song's opening is pretty good, but once it reaches its slightly anti-climactic *"Ooo-yeah, Ooo-yeah"* chorus, it just doesn't have the impact as some of the other tracks on the album.

#10 "Sorrow Is A Woman"

A decent mid-tempo song that also epitomizes how much Joe Elliott's distinct voice and vocal range strengthened over subsequent albums.

#9 "When The Walls Came Tumbling Down"

A pretty good song that has the ingredients of a great epic track, but you get the sense that the band was still feeling their way around to make it all work together, a feat they'll accomplish more effectively on future albums.

On a side note, the track's narration intro brings to mind Manowar's '80s song "Defender," which magnificently featured Orson Welles(!) handling the duties.

#8 "Rocks Off"

This very straightforward, guitar-driven deep track serves its purpose, complementing the other more memorable (impactful) rockers on the album.

#7 "Overture"

The other epic off of the *On Through The Night* album. It's moody and changes tempo, which works pretty well throughout. It's a respectable effort and an impressive accomplishment.

By the way, is anyone else reminded of Def Leppard's "Kings of the World" (bonus track on their live album *Mirror Ball*) at the 1:45 mark of "Overture"?

#6 "Hello America"

One of the most well-known Def Leppard songs from the band's early years.

It's a solid rock track that sufficiently introduced, figuratively and literally, what the band was all about to American audiences.

Not a bad first impression for a young band that's just coming into its own.

#5 "It Could Be You"

Though it's the album's shortest track (just over two and a

half minutes), "It Could Be You" stands out and packs a punch. Its tempo maintains a great energy throughout and effectively shifts into a slower gear right before reaching a memorable chorus.

#4 "Answer To The Master"

This song showcases the vast array of the band's budding talents: strong guitar riffs, solid melodies, and a rockin' guitar and drum solo.

The track also has a really good vibe, practically foreshadowing how the band will up the ante with their next album. That being said, "Answer To The Master" could have been included on the *High 'n' Dry* album and fit right in, with a sprinkle of Mutt Lange's production magic, of course.

#3 "It Don't Matter"

Another song with great rhythm; the arrangement effectively intertwines its melodic verses and driving drums throughout, leading to a rewarding, catchy chorus.

This is one of several tracks on *On Through The Night* that affirms Def Leppard's credibility as a legitimate, hard rock band with so much to offer.

#2 "Rock Brigade"

This straightforward, anthemic rocker offers up its share of goods, mixing melodies and hooks with hard-driving guitars and a catchy chorus.

It's understandable if this track brings to mind future Def Leppard songs "Stagefright" and "Rock! Rock! (Till You Drop)" off of the *Pyromania* album; "Rock Brigade" could easily be considered a precursor to those classics.

#1 "Wasted"

A powerful track that features a massive, instantly recognizable guitar riff, with hooks and melodies all leading to a fist-pumping chant of a chorus...*Wasted!*

It's worth noting the impressive guitar playing by Steve Clark and Pete Willis, not only on this track but throughout *On Through The Night*.

Album: *High 'n' Dry*

#10 "Lady Strange"

The only reason this track ranks tenth is because the *High 'n' Dry* album is filled with *many* other strong, hard-rockin' songs.

"Lady Strange" fits right in with the quality hard rock sound *High 'n' Dry* maintains throughout. It's guitar-driven and kicks into an (even more) accelerated gear at the song's midpoint, further showcasing the impressive talents of Steve Clark and Pete Willis.

#9 "No No No"

There is nothing subtle about this song.

Just hold on tight because this tune can be described as chaotic fun: it takes you on a wild ride, only slowing down briefly for its rip-roaring, powerful chorus.

#8 "High 'n' Dry (Saturday Night)"

This song periodically appears on Def Leppard's concert setlists. Sure, it's convenient to perform on a Saturday night, but a better reason is that it's still worthy of attention decades after its release.

It's classic early Leppard.

#7 "On Through The Night"

I always found it amusing that this track has the same name as the band's *previous* album.

Regardless of which album it ended up on, it's a really good song, filled with a lot of energy and a catchy hook. It slows down its rapid pace only for a moment, for what may be the band's most introspective lyrics, *"All we want to hear is the audience applause..."* By that point, they've got it.

#6 "Switch 625"

It's difficult to rank this track on its own, as it only feels right when it's paired up with "Bringin' On The Heartbreak." But since it is its own track on the album, it will be kept separate; even so, it's fitting and a coincidence that it also follows "Bringin' On The Heartbreak" in this ranking.

That aside, it's a great instrumental that spotlights Steve Clark's immense talents and, more broadly, his inimitable contributions to Def Leppard's music and sound -- on this album as well as all the other ones he would be part of.

#5 "Bringin' On The Heartbreak"

Did this ballad help contribute to MTV's popularity back in the '80s or was it the other way around?

Either way, the song became a success as MTV viewers were introduced to Def Leppard, musically *and* visually, many quickly becoming fans of the band.

The song provides *High 'n' Dry* with a well-deserved, albeit brief, slowdown from the rest of the album's non-stop, fast and furious pace.

By the way, for anyone lucky enough to see Def Leppard during the *Hysteria* tour, the flamenco-inspired acoustic introduction of "Bringin' On The Heartbreak" was not only outstanding but a refreshing take on the classic song, as it eventually kicked into a whole other gear, especially when Steve Clark and his twin-neck powered guitar took over.

#4 "Let It Go"

Another classic from the *High 'n' Dry* album that periodically makes an appearance at Def Leppard shows. It's yet another track that typifies what the band's sophomore album was all about: catchy, hard-rockin', power-chord-filled songs.

#3 "You Got Me Runnin'"

A track that exemplifies *High 'n' Dry*'s ability to masterfully infuse driving rhythms, melodies, and harmonies into a hard rock song.

"You Got Me Runnin" is also a prime example of how much Joe Elliott's vocals had strengthened since the *On Through The Night* album.

#2 "Another Hit And Run"

This song demonstrates how much Def Leppard upped their game and matured since their debut album.

"Another Hit And Run" is a potent, standout track that showcases the band's many talents as a unit: tight arrangements, crunchy guitar riffs, and driving drums complementing the song's verses, collectively building towards its powerful, shout-out-loud chorus...*Hit and run!*

#1 "Mirror Mirror (Look Into My Eyes)"

An excellent track that always seemed to be a bit under the radar on the *High 'n' Dry* album.

Songs like "Let It Go" and "High 'n' Dry" might immediately come to mind when you think of *High 'n' Dry's* rockers, but "Mirror Mirror (Look Into My Eyes)" deserves to be right up there, too.

The track's exemplary arrangement, featuring dueling guitars and infectious backing vocals, further proved how far Def Leppard songs had come since *On Through The Night*, and revealed how much more potential the band had.

Album: *Pyromania*

#10 "Comin' Under Fire"

Pyromania is a powerhouse of an album, appropriately titled in that it *crackles* with numerous classic Def Leppard songs. That said, "Comin' Under Fire" successfully serves its purpose as a solid deep track.

Though it's not *Pyromania*'s strongest offering, it plays an important part in making the album sizzle, and still be the dominant force that it is.

#9 "Die Hard The Hunter"

"Die Hard The Hunter" sounds great sonically, led by a powerful introduction comprised of war-like sound effects and synthesizers.

The song itself is satisfying, too, balancing verses with a memorable pre-chorus (and great guitar work), all complemented with its satisfactory chorus.

#8 "Billy's Got A Gun"

Another splendid deep track off of the *Pyromania* album.

Though it was never an official single, "Billy's Got A Gun" always connected well with fans (and concert audiences), simply because it's a very good song, structured well, catchy, and worthy of attention.

#7 "Action! Not Words"

The depth of *Pyromania* sometimes makes it easy to overlook some of the album's deep tracks, and that's the case with the underrated "Action! Not Words."

Big chorus, big hooks, and big guitars don't always apply to Def Leppard's deep tracks, but they satisfyingly do here.

#6 "Too Late For Love"

"Too Late For Love" spellbinds the moment you hear its classic opening sound effects.

The song's slow-and-steady pacing enhances and amplifies its overall arrangement, making the track all the more impactful and memorable.

#5 "Stagefright"

A great song and a crowd favorite, especially when it was used as a concert opener during Def Leppard's *Hysteria* tour.

The song's audience sound effect only amps up the electricity exuding from this high-voltage rocker.

#4 "Rock Of Ages"

Just about as anthemic as a Def Leppard song can get.

"Rock Of Ages" encapsulates what *Pyromania* represents in just over four minutes, most notably highlighted by its iconic call-to-arms chorus.

#3 "Foolin'"

I always found it interesting how most of *Pyromania*'s tracks feature distinct sound effects to introduce (and identify) a song before any music actually begins. The same applies here: You're instantly put into "Foolin'" mode before a guitar chord is struck!

The song's arrangement works extremely well, as momentum begins to build soon after Steve Clark's iconic guitar introduction, leading to an explosive and distinct stutter of a chorus.

#2 "Rock! Rock! (Till You Drop)"

Another song that showcases *Pyromania*'s sonically pleasing, bombastic, wall of sound production.

It's fitting that this is the album's opening track -- from its wailing lead vocals to rewarding chorus, it exhibits just how powerful a Def Leppard song can be. The song's *"Hold onto your hat"* opening line perfectly sums up what Def Leppard had in store for its fans with the almighty *Pyromania* album.

#1 "Photograph"

Just about as perfect as a Def Leppard song can get. "Photograph" is brimming with Steve Clark's signature guitar riffs (and an unforgettable guitar solo courtesy of newcomer at the time, Phil Collen), soaring vocals, and unforgettable stadium-sized harmonies.

The song *still* seems as potent and fresh today as when it was originally released.

Speaking of which, it's worth calling out again the massive sound sustained throughout *Pyromania*'s production courtesy of Mutt Lange. So much work went into making every single aspect sound absolutely perfect, all while coming across as straightforward rock and roll, pure and simple.

The same applies to "Photograph." Its intricate, multi-layered arrangement works beautifully, which makes hearing Joe Elliott's vocal-only version of the song (which can be found online) even more impressive, appreciated, and fascinating.

Album: *Hysteria*

#12 "Love And Affection"

If "Love Bites" wasn't included on *Hysteria*, this other "love" song might have ranked higher. It's a fine song, but it's on an album that's filled with so many other powerful tracks. As a result, "Love And Affection" is pushed further back in this ranking.

The song also works well as the album's final track, a pleasant cooldown from the exhilarating 62-minute workout *Hysteria* puts listeners' ears through.

#11 "Don't Shoot Shotgun"

Even though "Don't Shoot Shotgun" features big guitars and drums, catchy verses, and a memorable, melodic chorus, it can still be easily overlooked, even forgotten. Again, it's not because 'Shotgun' is weak, it's because it's among so many exceptional songs.

Having said that, it's a solid deep cut that leaves its own mark on *Hysteria*'s listening experience.

#10 "Excitable"

"Excitable" was Def Leppard's attempt at recording a rock song in the vein of Michael Jackson and Mick Jagger's track "State of Shock," which was quite popular when *Hysteria* was being recorded. There are some similarities between the two songs but "Excitable" has an appeal and identity all its own, including its classic "*Are you excitable?*" opening.

On a side note, some radio stations actually began playing "Excitable" after *Hysteria*'s seventh U.S. single ("Rocket") had finished its chart run back in 1989. "Excitable" would have made a fine eighth(!) single had it been officially released, yet another reminder of *Hysteria*'s extraordinary depth.

#9 "Run Riot"

An all-out rocker bursting with energy, so much so that it's over before you know it -- the fact that it is *Hysteria*'s shortest track has nothing to do with it!

#8 "Rocket"

"*Guitar!*" and "*Drums!*" work very well together on this massive-sounding, sonically-pleasing track.

Toss in a bunch of references to music icons and a soaring

middle section (that literally sounds like it's soaring) to go with its spectacular production, and you have a Def Leppard song that still towers to this day.

#7 "Armageddon It"

Don't be fooled by the #7 ranking, as this song is one of many great tracks on *Hysteria*.

"Armageddon It" bristles with sensational hooks and memorable rhythm, not to mention an excellent sing-along chorus.

#6 "Love Bites"

Def Leppard's most successful ballad which can also be considered the band's biggest hit, since it reached #1 on *Billboard*'s Hot 100 singles chart (though an argument can be made that "Pour Some Sugar On Me" was a *bigger* hit, and had a greater impact).

Nevertheless, "Love Bites" remains a sentimental favorite for many, with its catchy harmonies still resonating in a lot of fans' ears.

#5 "Women"

A great opening track for *Hysteria*. Its big, powerful sound, and explosive, fist-in-the-air chorus leave a lasting impression that splendidly sets the tone for the rest of the songs that follow.

Even though "Women" dramatically underperformed as a single, it's still a unique, bold, and effective rocker.

#4 "Gods Of War"

As powerful as some Def Leppard songs can be, they still bow down to this classic epic.

Piling on hook after hook, "Gods Of War" continually intensifies until it spills into its almighty, rewarding chorus. It's an unforgettable track.

The band used to say they were aiming for "*Star Wars* for the ears" during *Hysteria*'s production, and they certainly achieved it here. And even though the song's political soundbites are now several decades old, they can still be chill-inducing, especially in how the band (and Mutt Lange) integrated them into the track's exceptional finale.

#3 "Pour Some Sugar On Me"

A bombastic, rock powerhouse.

"Pour Some Sugar On Me" is a monster of a song -- as in monster drums, guitars, and hooks -- led by its gruff, rap-infused, sing-along lead vocals. Combine all of these elements, and you have one iconic result.

If there ever was a late '80s rock anthem, hands down, this is it.

Often imitated (and arguably ripped off by other acts) but never duplicated.

#2 "Animal"

Simply put, "Animal" is one of the band's premier mid-tempo rockers, and similar to "Photograph," it's about as perfect as a Def Leppard song can get.

It's easy to sometimes overlook this gem of a track due to the numerous hit songs on *Hysteria*, but "Animal" remains some of the best music the band has ever recorded.

#1 "Hysteria"

Some Def Leppard songs have the ability to transport you to a different time and place the very moment you hear their opening notes; "Hysteria" unfailingly achieves this remarkable feat.

Its meticulous arrangement, hypnotic rhythm, and infectious melody work together beautifully, resulting in this unforgettable, tremendous song.

It remains such a magical mysteria to this day.

Album: *Adrenalize*

#10 "Tonight"

Terrific guitar intro. Pretty good verse structure and bridge. The chorus? It's...okay.

What usually makes a Def Leppard chorus special is when it elevates a song to greater heights, eclipsing everything that preceded it and rewarding listeners for taking the music journey.

The chorus for "Tonight" falls short of having that extra something to take the song over the top.

I know many fans *really* like the song, and by no means am I saying it's bad, but let's broaden out this discussion a bit more for just a moment.

I have very fond memories of *Adrenalize*, including waiting in line to purchase my CD copy one minute after midnight the day it was released. It had been many years since the release of *Hysteria*, and so refreshing to finally hear a new album of Def Leppard songs.

I also remember reading a local music critic's negative review of the album the week of its release. Basically, the review said *Adrenalize*'s multi-layered production was too overproduced, not only taking most of the emotion out of its songs' harmonies but also making choruses sound like they were recorded in a vacuum.

I dismissed the review back then, and still don't completely agree with it now, but I must admit the observation does ring true at times when listening to *Adrenalize*, especially with "Tonight" and its chorus.

This topic will come up again in this ranking, so I'll wrap things up for now by saying many other Def Leppard ballads work more effectively than "Tonight," such as "Love Bites," "Bringin' On The Heartbreak," and "Two Steps Behind."

It might be a coincidence, but the three other ballads I just mentioned have something else in common: Def Leppard still performs them on tour.

Aside from the *Adrenalize* tour, the band rarely, if ever, performs "Tonight" in concert.

I wonder why.

#9 "Personal Property"

A fine deep track, with a jam-packed lyric-filled chorus that's as fun as it is a mental exercise to sing along to.

#8 "Heaven Is"

A straight-up, Def Leppard pop song that's ultimately...pretty good.

"Heaven Is" most definitely has its share of hooks (upon hooks), huge power chords, and big harmonies.

That being said, "Heaven Is" seems to give the impression that the band was feeling the mounting pressure of following up *Hysteria*'s success, and tried their darndest to outperform it by stacking an overabundance of hooks, layer upon gigantic layer, wherever possible.

It's understandable: they were out of the spotlight for many years, lost an integral part of the band with Steve Clark's passing, were recording the album as a four-piece, didn't have Mutt Lange to produce it, and the music industry had changed so much since *Hysteria*'s heyday. There certainly was a lot of pressure to deal with.

Those seemingly insurmountable odds always come to mind when listening to "Heaven Is" -- the band overcompensating, trying to (unnecessarily) make the song sound as abundantly pleasing to the ear and as radio-friendly as possible.

Back to my earlier comments about "Tonight" and the music critic's "vacuum" reference. At times, it can also apply to "Heaven Is," among other *Adrenalize* tracks like "I Wanna Touch U," "Have You Ever Needed Someone So Bad," and "Stand Up (Kick Love Into Motion)." Their choruses, while excellent, sometimes tend to sound a little too sleek for their own good, almost otherworldly, which may work in one sense but detracts in another.

Even though these are my views, I would like to add that I found Rick Savage's candid opinion about *Adrenalize*, decades after its release, revealing.

Sav's comments were included in Def Leppard's 2015 *Classic Rock Presents* Fanpack:

> "We ended up making a record by the numbers... We tried to outdo 'Hysteria,' which was a mistake...It doesn't really cut it for me."

Joe Elliott also reflected on his conflicted opinion of *Adrenalize* in recent years:

"My opinion of the album changes depending on which way the wind's blowing. I mean, sometimes I really don't like it, and then there's other times I think 'No, that's our glam rock album, we made a really cool record.'"

#7 "Make Love Like A Man"

A fun Def Leppard song, whether heard on *Adrenalize* or performed live in concert.

It's over-simplistic but a good time, from the moment it begins all the way to its Led Zeppelin-ish "Whole Lotta Love" guitar riff at the song's end.

Kudos to Phil Collen for doing a great impression of Joe Elliott when he briefly takes over the lead vocals.

#6 "I Wanna Touch U"

Huge drums, grandiose guitars, and a super-catchy melody. The same can be said about "Pour Some Sugar On Me" (among other Def Leppard songs), as it's easy to think of "I Wanna Touch U' as a pseudo-sequel to 'Sugar.'

I've already mentioned the (potential) ramifications of *Adrenalize's* polished production, so here's an alternative thought: Wouldn't it have been interesting if "I Wanna Touch U" was recorded during the band's *High 'n' Dry* or *Pyromania* era? It's intriguing to contemplate what a more raw version of the song would have sounded like.

#5 "Tear It Down"

A great Def Leppard song.

One caveat: If a more bare-bones, hard rock version of "Tear It Down" hadn't already existed (the B-side to the "Women" single), this refresh wouldn't have sounded somewhat watered down compared to the original.

#4 "Have You Ever Needed Someone So Bad"

A Def Leppard power ballad that satisfies.

Its arrangement -- highlighted by a superb pre-chorus, not to mention a rewarding sing-along chorus -- works splendidly in making this ballad soar.

#3 "White Lightning"

Adrenalize's great epic.

The song can be referenced as the album's "Gods of War," but "White Lightning" is much too good to be dismissed as such.

The track also bears the somber reminder of Steve Clark's passing ("white lightning" was allegedly one of Steve's nicknames on stage), and that Def Leppard had forever been changed.

#2 "Stand Up (Kick Love Into Motion)"

A wonderful, moody Def Leppard song.

If you were to try to come up with parallels between *Adrenalize* and *Hysteria*, "Stand Up (Kick Love Into Motion)" would be this album's "Hysteria" track. That's not to say 'Stand Up' is a copycat; it's actually a compliment, though this underrated song never received the notoriety it deserved.

#1 "Let's Get Rocked"

This Def Leppard song features many of the band's signature offerings. Being the first single off of *Adrenalize*, it needed to, as it also marked the band's long-awaited return.

Humorous lyrics aside, "Let's Get Rocked" sounded different and refreshing when it was originally released, especially as radio stations began to shift their airplay focus to alternative music.

It's not surprising that this catchy, feel-good track remains a fan favorite and a staple on Def Leppard's setlists. Heck, any song that can successfully incorporate Beethoven's Fifth Symphony into its driving beat is worthy of repeated listens.

Album: *Slang*

#11 "Breathe A Sigh"

A Def Leppard song with a Boyz II Men R&B vibe -- not a description you hear very often.

As a one-off, it's an intriguing effort. It certainly has its share of pleasing melodies, but it's a fair song overall.

On an amusing note, I'm reminded of how Joe Elliott's vocal at the song's 2:25 mark sounded to some like he was saying, "*I mow the lawn for your affection.*" Obviously, that's not the case, but it would have been interesting if it was -- with "lawn" referencing back to the last album's "Let's Get Rocked" line "*Mow the lawn!*" The priorities of that song's "average, ordinary everyday kid" evolved now that he's a little older and lovestruck (in "Breathe A Sigh"); now *that* would be some impressive song-to-song continuity!

#10 "Truth?"

This song always seemed a bit forced, like the band was attempting to take on the ever-growing alternative music movement happening at the time and making a conscious effort to record a Nine Inch Nails-type song.

Its industrial music vibe is fine and achieves what the band set out to do, but it's okay if it still makes you long for Def Leppard's trademark sound when listening to it.

#9 "Gift Of Flesh"

This hard-rocking, guitar-driven song effectively and reassuringly injects Def Leppard's brand of rock into what could be considered the band's most "non-Def Leppard" album.

#8 "Work It Out"

This fine song was written by Vivian Campbell, before being "Leppard-ized." It has a good tempo but the rewarding Def Leppard chorus many would expect never seems to arrive.

Slang was an album that intentionally went in a different creative direction, and while it includes quite a few great tracks, "Work It Out" lands in the middle of the spectrum.

#7 "Slang"

An admirable song effort, as the band attempted to try something different yet again.

While "Slang" is far from being one of the band's best songs, I discovered a whole new appreciation for it after seeing Def Leppard perform it live multiple times. It had a whole new energy and vibe that was actually more appealing to me than the song's album version.

#6 "Deliver Me"

"Deliver Me" arguably has the sound and feel of a *Pyromania* deep cut, and that's not a bad thing.

It sounds more raw and edgy than your typical Def Leppard song, but the same can be said about its dark lyrics and solemn mood. Put it all together and you get a fairly satisfying track.

By the way, if you'd like to further appreciate the song's production, listen to the first 20 seconds of "Deliver Me" with only your right speaker on (turn off your left speaker). Enjoy, Joe Elliott fans!

#5 "Turn To Dust"

An underrated track that features massive-sounding guitars weaving perfectly in and out of the song's verses. It's an impressive arrangement that leads into a solid chorus.

"Turn To Dust" is one of Def Leppard's more unique songs and even though it isn't as well known as the band's more popular hits, it's absolutely worth a listen...over and over again.

#4 "Pearl Of Euphoria"

Slowly paced and moody, this intense track features big drums as well as dueling guitars that showcase the talents of Phil Collen and Vivian Campbell.

It all comes together well to complement this epic song's powerful lyrics and vocals.

#3 "Blood Runs Cold"

One of the best songs from the *Slang* album, this emotional track melodically mesmerizes from start to finish.

Knowing that it's inspired by gone-but-never-forgotten guitarist Steve Clark makes this melancholy song all the more heartfelt and powerful.

#2 "Where Does Love Go When It Dies"

"Where Does Love Go When It Dies" is a magnificent track, filled with sensational melodies, excellent lyrics, and so much more. It's thoroughly satisfying.

This underrated song shines a light on the band's more experimental side while also representing all the best things Def Leppard has to offer.

It should not be overlooked.

#1 "All I Want Is Everything"

If you put aside commercial success and chart performance, and only focused on genuine quality, "All I Want Is Everything" would deserve to be included on the list of Def Leppard's greatest song compositions.

Lyrically, one of their best. Vocally, the raw emotion is felt throughout.

It's an exceptional song, plain and simple. Referring to this stripped-down gem as either "plain" or "simple," though, would be an injustice.

Album: *Euphoria*

#13 "Disintegrate"

A fine guitar instrumental.

Even if "Disintegrate" was considered a more contemporary version of "Switch 625" -- which comes to mind when listening to this track -- it doesn't leave the same lasting impression.

#12 "Day After Day"

Take *Pyromania*'s "Too Late For Love," mix in a little (slower-paced) "Die Hard The Hunter," throw in a bit of *High 'n' Dry*'s "Mirror Mirror (Take A Look Into My Eyes)," and you get something along the lines of "Day After Day."

The difference is that all three of the older songs referenced easily stand on their own. "Day After Day" on the other hand sounds more like an attempt to replicate music from an earlier era; hence, the end result just doesn't sound as authentic as those previous songs, nor does it have its own identity.

#11 "It's Only Love"

This song's pop-lite approach seems better suited for the *X* album than *Euphoria*.

Maybe it's the easy-listening *"Na na na na na na na na na..."* lyrics, but it sounds like the band is holding back and not allowing themselves to really let loose; a little more Leppard "oomph" would have been beneficial and made a difference.

The song's pre-chorus has appeal, but it doesn't make up for what ends up being a fairly standard track.

#10 "Guilty"

"Guilty" sounds somewhat like a cross between "Hysteria" and (a bit of) "Animal."

The song itself is okay, though its *"If you mean [interchangeable noun]..."* chorus becomes a little too repetitive.

By the way, remember the portion near the end of Def Leppard's song "Animal," beginning with *"Take me, Tame me, Make me your animal..."*? That part always comes to mind when reaching the 3:14 mark of "Guilty" -- just replace *"Guil-ty, Guil-ty..."* with those lyrics from "Animal."

Just saying.

#9 "All Night"

A funky Prince-esque Def Leppard song. Hmm.

It's a respectable effort, but the song arguably would have been more appealing if it were *more* in the vein of Def Leppard.

Case in point, "Pour Some Sugar On Me" brought rap into Def Leppard's universe, and the band created something all their own with it. "All Night" ultimately sounds more like a Prince song than a Def Leppard song, and that shouldn't be the case.

#8 "Kings Of Oblivion"

This song has an *On Through The Night* (album *and* song) type of feel to it. It also could have fit right in as a *Pyromania* deep track.

Comparisons aside, "Kings of Oblivion" has some really good energy and a finely crafted, catchy chorus.

#7 "Goodbye"

A decent ballad featuring a nice melody and appealing verses, but its chorus falls a bit short and loses some momentum, especially due to its plethora of lyrics.

#6 "21st Century Sha La La La Girl"

Bursting with energy, this catchy song is loads of fun. The lyric *"Cosmic sugar high"* fittingly describes this "caffeinated," vibrant track.

"21st Century Sha La La La Girl" is a really good time.

#5 "To Be Alive"

A splendid track brought forward by Vivian Campbell that can easily be overlooked due to Def Leppard's deep and robust catalog. This song's distinct, harmonious arrangement features wonderful melodies and is capped off with a heartfelt guitar solo that truly shines.

#4 "Paper Sun"

This track is worthy of joining the ranks of significant Def Leppard epics like "Gods of War" and "White Lightning."

"Paper Sun" is a solid standout, and one of the best songs *Euphoria* has to offer.

#3 "Back In Your Face"

A vintage Def Leppard song reminiscent of Gary Glitter's "Rock and Roll Part 2."

Filled with whimsical lyrics and a playful, boisterous attitude, "Back In Your Face" is lively and surprisingly impactful.

You get the sense the band had a lot of fun recording this track, which makes it all the more enjoyable to listen to.

Intentional or not, "Back In Your Face" also has a *Pyromania* vibe to it. And that's not only because the sinister laugh from Joe Elliott at the song's 1:17 mark very much resembles his laugh on "Rock Of Ages" (at the 2:00 mark).

#2 "Demolition Man"

A rapid, intense song with a deliriously fun, brisk chorus that brings to mind Sweet's "Ballroom Blitz."

"Demolition Man" is a great rocker that's truly underrated and worthy of a lot more attention.

#1 "Promises"

Def Leppard's signature sound is best showcased on this great track.

"Promises" is catchy, filled with hooks in all the right places, and has a rewarding chorus. With that in mind, it's not a coincidence that Mutt Lange was involved in the song's creation.

I recall how some press coverage initially compared "Promises" to "Photograph," which wasn't fair, as "Promises" doesn't have the same heft as the *Pyromania* classic. Maybe, at best, it's more of a pop-lite version of "Photograph," but a better comparison nowadays would be to a track on the band's self-titled *Def Leppard* album, which we'll get to in just a bit.

Album: *X*

#13 "Scar"

The song's opening guitars sound like an edgier version of *Euphoria's* "Guilty" opening.

"Scar" mellows out soon afterward but kicks into gear when it reaches a chorus that once again evokes "Guilty": The repetitious *"All that you [interchangeable verb]"* chorus from "Scar" corresponds with the *"If you mean [interchangeable noun]"* chorus from "Guilty."

All in all, "Scar" has a bit of an identity crisis.

#12 "Girl Like You"

The solid guitar riffs complementing the song's verses bring to mind *Slang's* superior track "Turn To Dust."

"Girl Like You" features an appealing melody but doesn't capitalize on it once it reaches its rather lackluster chorus, which also sounds somewhat out of place and disconnected from the rest of the song.

#11 "Love Don't Lie"

"Love Don't Lie" fits right in with the *X* album's pop-lite fare, but it's fairly standard when compared to some of the album's stronger tracks.

#10 "Gravity"

A song that's more on the experimental side, not that there's anything wrong with that.

It's uncommon for a Def Leppard song to not include a guitar solo, but that is the case with this track and its unique dance-pop arrangement.

In the end, it's a decent, respectable effort. But frankly, Def Leppard's "Gravity" demo/alternate version titled "Perfect Girl" is more appealing and would have been a better fit for *X*.

#9 "Cry"

"Cry" has several positive attributes, including a really strong, engaging opening, but every time it starts to build momentum, it hits the brakes -- literally, the song stops -- right before launching into a chorus that not only seems disjointed from everything that preceded it but also doesn't serve the song very well. (This topic will be revisited in the *Songs from the Sparkle Lounge* song ranking.)

#8 "Let Me Be The One"

A fine pop song. There's nothing wrong with it, but after hearing the band's original demo -- which included piano, strings, and sounded quite Beatlesque -- it makes you wish the band would have put *that* version on the album instead.

#7 "You're So Beautiful"

A pretty good song, but Def Leppard's mastery of melody almost works against them here, as "You're So Beautiful" is overloaded with an abundance of hooks (upon hooks), perhaps to its detriment.

The hooks in and of themselves serve their purpose. But collectively, they begin to compete against -- instead of complement -- each other.

The end result is a song that doesn't feel quite whole.

Remember the Def Leppard lyric "*a little too much could never be enough now*" from "I Wanna Touch U"? Well, in this instance, a little too much is actually a little too much.

#6 "Long Long Way To Go"

One of a couple of tracks on the *X* album not written by the band. Regardless, this heartfelt song succeeds and effectively showcases emotional lyrics, strong vocals, and melodies galore.

#5 "Now"

A solid track that features more of a modern rock sound and isn't your typical Def Leppard song.

In the end, "Now" fits right in with the rest of the *X* album, and does it well.

#4 "Four Letter Word"

This song not only sounds great (and AC/DC-ish), it has a raw, edgy feel, and a confident attitude throughout.

The track would have felt right at home if it were included on the *High 'n' Dry* album; it has that kind of vintage Def Leppard vibe.

#3 "Unbelievable"

Even though "Unbelievable" wasn't written by the band, the song is impressive and has Def Leppard's stamp all over it.

It's a melodically-pleasing ballad with an infectious, soaring chorus that works extremely well.

#2 "Everyday"

Nowhere near as popular as other Def Leppard deep tracks, but this mid-tempo rocker is not only solid, it's one of the best deep cuts the band has recorded in the 2000s.

#1 "Torn To Shreds"

One of Def Leppard's most underrated songs, and that comment doesn't only apply to the *X* album.

This excellent track features an explosive chorus and massive harmonies, both of which arguably rival the best hooks the band has ever created -- and that's saying a lot!

With a running time of less than three minutes, this gem (and its memorable chorus, which might oh-so-subtly bring to mind the chorus from the '80s classic "In A Big Country") is over before you know it and always leaves you wanting more.

"Torn To Shreds" is one of Def Leppard's best songs to never have been a single.

Album: *Songs From The Sparkle Lounge*

#11 "Hallucinate"

The song gets off to a promising start, with what sounds like a spirited jam session, and builds nicely while showcasing Joe Elliott's gravelly vocals and its share of guitar riffs and hooks.

Unfortunately, its momentum fizzles out at the chorus and veers the song off course, similar to the *X* album's "Cry."

Let me expand on this for a moment.

Sometimes Def Leppard creates a song by "gluing" together (i.e., connecting) ideas that are independent of each other. This isn't my opinion; it's what the band has stated numerous times over the years, as it's part of their creative process.

Basically, one band member has an unfinished song idea, which ends up being pieced together with a completely separate song idea from another member, and so on. Over time, and with some creative maneuvering, the individual portions come together to create a new song.

The song "Hysteria" is a great example; Rick Savage and Phil Collen combined separate song ideas they had each been working on, which eventually became the song's foundation.

This type of technique inevitably comes to mind when listening to certain tracks from the band's later albums; they have the makings of being *really* good songs but lose their momentum along the way, sometimes to the point of sounding disjointed. The thought comes to mind when listening to songs like "Hallucinate" and "Cry," especially when reaching their respective choruses.

Now, were different song ideas actually stitched together in those instances? Maybe, maybe not. But just when you think you're on the brink of hearing the next great Def Leppard classic, it ultimately ends up being a, um, very deep track.

#10 "Bad Actress"

A straightforward rocker that ventures into Robert Plant territory -- at various points throughout the song, you just want to sing along while using Plant's "Tall Cool One" lyric *"Lighten up, baby, I'm in love with you...!"*

"Bad Actress" is also in the vein of Def Leppard's superior (B-side) "She's Too Tough," ultimately sounding more like a B-side itself.

#9 "Come Undone"

The song has a great build-up and features some very good guitar riffs, which are also reminiscent of the ones in "Cry."

Unfortunately, the chorus doesn't complement the rest of the song, as the payoff just isn't there. (The comments included with "Hallucinate" also apply here.)

#8 "Only The Good Die Young"

An appealing start, but just as you get your hopes up that the song will kick into a higher gear, it falls short: the gratifying Def Leppard chorus you feel like you're being guided to and eagerly awaiting doesn't arrive.

Overall, the song is okay with *a lot* of untapped potential.

#7 "Nine Lives"

Def Leppard and Tim McGraw join forces, and the result is...okay.

Putting aside the rock and country collaboration, the song features some of Def Leppard's signature attributes, most notably during its appealing, melodic pre-chorus.

But once you get past the twangy guitar intro (which brings to mind the guitar intro from "Armageddon It"), its elementary lyrics and shouting chorus make for a rather standard track overall.

#6 "Cruise Control"

A solid, gritty song further heightened by a hypnotic rhythm and wailing guitars; at first, the track comes across as a more melodic version of "Truth?" from the *Slang* album.

It would have been nice, though, if the band let loose on "Cruise Control" and took more risks, especially during its subdued chorus, but it's still pleasing and works well.

#5 "Gotta Let It Go"

The Cult's "Fire Woman" comes to mind when hearing this song's opening guitars, but "Gotta Let It Go" stands on its own, as it simmers throughout its effectual verses and pre-chorus, finally boiling over into an explosively good, driving chorus.

By the way, the three successive, rapid-fire guitar licks at the end of the song bring to mind the ending of *Pyromania's* "Billy's Got a Gun" (at "Billy's" 4:54 mark, before the drum loop portion begins).

#4 "Love"

An emotionally charged ballad that exhibits exceptional vocals and excellent guitars.

Yes, it's Queen-like -- its arrangement even echoes Queen's song, "Jealousy" -- but "Love" is also unlike any other Def Leppard power ballad, which is refreshing.

"Love" could have been one of Def Leppard's greatest epics but has always seemed slightly incomplete. Including an additional verse (or more) to the song's second half would have provided more richness and balance to its overall arrangement.

Nevertheless, the song's first half is nearly perfect and works magnificently.

#3 "Go"

"Go" is a very satisfying, energy-filled surprise. Its heavy, driving rhythm doesn't let up, and what could be mistaken as a bland chorus on paper (*"Go! Just Go! Just Go!"*) works out splendidly.

The song overachieves in many ways and is worthy of being the album's opening track.

#2 "Tomorrow"

Joe Elliott's *"Whoo whoo whoo..."* opening vocals might remind some of Bono's on the U2 track "Elevation," but this Def Leppard song has much more to offer beyond that.

"Tomorrow" is one of *Songs from the Sparkle Lounge's* hidden gems. And just like "Everyday" from the *X* album, "Tomorrow" is a lesser-known, underrated track that makes a great impression and resonates, if only given a chance.

#1 "C'mon C'mon"

This song could be considered a descendant of the *Euphoria* track "Back In Your Face," as they're both big, crowd-pleasing arena rocking anthems in the spirit of "Rock and Roll Part 2."

The song has an excellent groove, catchy verses, driving guitars, and a great pre-chorus. The chorus itself is sufficient, though it might have been even more impactful if it wasn't simply the song's title being repeated incessantly.

That said, "C'mon C'mon" is an album standout and a rockin' track that captures the essence of Def Leppard, and what the band does best.

Album: *Def Leppard*

#14 "Blind Faith"

The delivery of the lead vocal from this decent deep cut brings to mind "Deliver Me." While "Blind Faith" lacks that *Slang* track's grandiose chorus, it might have been more riveting if it had one of its own. When given the chance, "Blind Faith" goes in a more mellow direction instead, holding back its firepower until the song's final minute.

#13 "Energized"

Ironically, even though it's titled "Energized," the song itself is somewhat, well, low energy.

"Energized" is actually a pretty good track, but it lacks the kinetic intensity that could have supercharged it and added more fuel to its fire. In other words, "energized" it more.

#12 "Forever Young"

What sounds like a freeform jam session at first evolves into a compelling track that periodically exhibits *High 'n' Dry*'s raw sound and attitude.

The lead vocals come off as spontaneous the way they are sung over pervasive guitars and hard-driving drums, yet everything melds together nicely just in time for the song's spirited chorus.

#11 "Man Enough"

I appreciate the effort that went into "Man Enough," and the "Another One Bites The Dust" disco vibe it brings to mind (thanks to Sav's cool, omnipresent bass-line groove). But the track seems mostly stuck in first gear, which results in the song sounding a little too repetitious for its own good.

#10 "Battle Of My Own"

Blend some folk-blues music with a big dose of Led Zeppelin added halfway in, and this is the Def Leppard song you get.

Overall, it's a pretty good track that jams throughout and exemplifies the *Def Leppard* album's diverse offerings.

#9 "Wings Of An Angel"

The first 30 seconds of "Wings Of An Angel" includes a portion that's reminiscent of The Cult's "Fire Woman" (yes, "Gotta Let It Go" had a similar reference), while the song's vocals can be described as a cross between "Deliver Me" and "Too Late For Love."

That said, the song's verses are solid and impactful, as they lead into a decent pre-chorus and chorus.

Similar to previous comments (see "Hallucinate"), there are times when "Wings Of An Angel" sounds a bit "stitched" together, most notably at the pre-chorus. Not saying it is, but it comes across that way.

#8 "Invincible"

The song gets off to a fine start with a driving rhythm that evokes memories of A-ha's "Take On Me" (without the keyboards).

Despite a fair chorus that becomes a little repetitious the further you get into the song, "Invincible" is still a pretty good track.

By the way, the last 20 or so seconds of "Invincible" (starting at the song's 3:25 mark) bring to mind the final moments of *Hysteria*'s "Run Riot," to the point you practically expect Joe Elliott to wrap up "Invincible" by belting out his "Run Riot" signature lines: *"I'll take you from your misery! Come on! Stick with me!"*

#7 "Sea Of Love"

Another Def Leppard song you wouldn't normally expect to hear from the band.

"Sea Of Love" maintains a different kind of energy and vibe throughout that might catch some fans off guard. That's not a negative, though, as the song still features some rockin' verses and a satisfying, catchy chorus.

#6 "Last Dance"

This song's acoustic guitar opening might remind some younger listeners of the Britney Spears song "Chillin' With You." Maybe it's just me, but Britney's *"You!"* opening lyric could fit pretty darn well into this song's guitar intro. (Ok, a much better coincidental parallel might be the opening guitar in Pink Floyd's "Goodbye Blue Sky" and the song "Hysteria.")

Nevertheless, "Last Dance" is a lovely little number that builds dramatically the further you get into it. It's a good, straightforward album track.

By the way, is anyone else reminded of Poison's "Every Rose Has Its Thorn" near the end of "Last Dance's" great guitar solo (at about the 2:45 mark)? Ok, I digress.

#5 "Broke 'N' Brokenhearted"

A fun, rockin' track whose sound and attitude conjure up thoughts of the *High 'n' Dry* album.

It's definitely more raw compared to other tracks on the *Def Leppard* album, sounding as if it was recorded on the fly, which is intended as a compliment to the song's edgy feel.

The song's gruffness also brings to mind Billy Joel's "You May Be Right" -- the band could belt out Joel's classic *"You may be right!"* chorus at any moment throughout the song, and it would fit right in.

"Broke 'N' Brokenhearted" is a good time.

#4 "Let's Go"

A Def Leppard song that figuratively screams "We're back!" (as the band intended), and the reason why it was chosen to be the

Def Leppard album's first single.

"Let's Go" instantly reminds listeners of the band's capabilities and trademark sound, beginning with its "Pour Some Sugar On Me"-like guitar opening.

The song's slower pace is impactful and serves an intentional purpose, but a brisker tempo might have added more urgency and vigor to the overall arrangement.

#3 "All Time High"

"All Time High" is one of the most underrated tracks on the *Def Leppard* album.

This splendid, energetic rocker would also have been extremely effective as a show opener for the *Def Leppard* album tour. (Sorry "Let's Go.")

Not only would "All Time High" have offered an even more vigorous start to the concert, but it also would have provided a great opportunity to introduce audiences to some of Def Leppard's *other* great, new songs (i.e., offer yet another reason to buy the *Def Leppard* album, above and beyond its few "singles").

Go ahead, play the song's first minute or so, while imagining a jam-packed, frenzied concert arena. The venue's lights go out, "All Time High" begins to play, and the curtain falls soon after. It would be exhilarating and memorable.

#2 "Dangerous"

Similar to "Let's Go," "Dangerous" is prone to conjure up some memories of Def Leppard songs from an earlier era.

Trademark guitar licks, solid verses, and a pretty good pre-chorus, all build up to an undeniably catchy chorus.

"Dangerous" is much sleeker compared to the band's older material, but it does have moments that will likely bring to mind *Pyromania*, as well as "Promises" off of the *Euphoria* album.

#1 "We Belong"

Not only a great track but a unique one, being the first (and only) time every Def Leppard band member gets to sing lead vocals. It's an effective approach and adds an extra layer of genuine emotion (and perspective) to the song.

The song's excellent lyrics are worth noting, too, as are Joe Elliott's understated, yet moving vocals.

"We Belong" packs a subtle wallop that's unforgettable.

Some Def Leppard Trivia

After going through all 115 tracks above, here's some additional information for your amusement.

Number Of Songs That Included The Word "Love" In Their Title: 10

- "Too Late For Love"
- "Love And Affection"
- "Love Bites"
- "Make Love Like A Man"
- "Stand Up (Kick Love Into Motion)"
- "Where Does Love Go When It Dies"
- "It's Only Love"
- "Love Don't Lie"
- "Love"
- "Sea Of Love"

Number Of Songs That Included The Word "Rock" (In Some Shape Or Form) In Their Title: 6*

- "Rocks Off"
- "Rock Brigade"
- "Rock Of Ages"
- "Rock Rock (Till You Drop)"
- "Let's Get Rocked"
- "Rocket" (*Sure, this one may not count, but I'm reminded of how some publications used to incorrectly refer to the song as "Rock It" when it was a new release.)

Number Of Songs That Include A Female Reference In Their Title: 6

- "Sorrow Is A Woman
- "Lady Strange"
- "Women"
- "21st Century Sha La La La Girl"
- "Girl Like You"
- "Bad Actress"

Number Of Songs That Include A Male Reference In Their Title: 5

- "Billy's Got A Gun"
- "Make Love Like A Man"
- "Kings Of Oblivion"
- "Demolition Man"

- "Man Enough"

Final Thoughts

There you have it.

Again, I have no doubt this ranking has its fair share of fans who vehemently disagree, but that's what is so appealing about the band's music: there are so many great songs to choose from to satisfy diverse music tastes!

KEEP INDULGING IN DEF LEPPARD!

DefLeppardReport.com

Printed in Great Britain
by Amazon